T0084015

Advance Pr[
Crisis of Responsibility

"David has hit home on the key point that must drive a new era of prosperity: with greater opportunity comes greater responsibility. The next generation of climbers in an aspirational society deserve a better shake from the establishment, but ultimately, they must embrace all challenges with a dogged determination. David's book says no to the blame game, and yes to the triumph of the human spirit."

–ANTHONY SCARAMUCCI, former White House Communications Director; Founder, SkyBridge Capital

"There is a virtuous cycle between responsibility and prosperity, and David has tapped into this favorite message of Jack Kemp in a way we need today more than ever. The vicious cycle of deteriorating social structures and poverty can be replaced, and readers of this book will see the path forward for real growth—a virtuous, opportunity-oriented society."

–LARRY KUDLOW, Senior Contributor, CNBC

"Only when the great mass of people reawaken to their civic duties will they be able to wrest control of America from an elite that has shown its failure to lead again and again. David Bahnsen's new book is the first step along this important path."

–JONAH GOLDBERG, Senior Fellow and Contributor, *National Review*

"David Bahnsen outlines cultural, economic, and political remedies for an ailing America of all classes. His often autobiographical message is that our fate still rests in our own hands. We are not pawns of global determinism, but with a few basic collective reforms and a return to individual self-reliance instead of our current self-obsessions, we can rebuild a prosperous, fair, and dynamic American culture and civilization. An outsider/insider message of hope and renewal that is now as rare as it is needed."

–VICTOR DAVIS HANSON, Senior Fellow, the Hoover Institution, Stanford University

"David Bahnsen has written a bracing and incisive critique of our increasingly pervasive culture of victimization. He makes a compelling case that it's still within our power, and absolutely necessary, that we help ourselves. You will enjoy and profit from this book."

–RICH LOWRY, Editor in Chief, *National Review*

"When will we put our fingers to better use than pointing them at each other or thrusting a middle one into the air? David Bahnsen shows us how to use our hands and brains to improve housing, education, labor markets, tax policy, and more."

–DR. MARVIN OLASKY, Editor in Chief, WORLD

"In any debate, the one who controls the narrative wins the day, and David Bahnsen is about shifting the narrative on discussions related to doing well and good at the same time. Bahnsen has undertaken this herculean task in Crisis of Responsibility by combining his economic and financial acumen with his moral clarity in a manner that is neither didactic nor preachy. See if you don't agree."

–FR. ROBERT SIRICO, President, the Acton Institute

"We all look for paths for finances and economics to help us succeed and move ahead in life. David Bahnsen has targeted the best possible stance toward this, which is to take responsibility for one's actions, starting at the individual level. He also provides a well-thought-out framework of specific suggestions to get this done. Highly recommended."

–DR. JOHN TOWNSEND, *New York Times* bestselling author; Founder of the Townsend Institute for Leadership and Counseling

"The philosopher Johann Herder once defined culture as 'the lifeblood of a people; the flow of moral energy that keeps a society intact.' If that analysis is correct, then we can respond that our society has been definitively exsanguinated. For this reason, I am so glad David Bahnsen's book has made its way to the public—for such a time as this. From Wall Street to Main Street and from tech to trade, Bahnsen diagnoses the fundamental problem that ails us and prescribes the only possible cure. He chronicles the decline of individual responsibility while simultaneously offering concrete proposals to bring it back to the nation."

–DR. GREGORY THORNBURY, President, King's College

"*Markets are living moral creatures, as David Bahnsen notes. The world has been waiting for someone from finance to address the moral aspect of the 2008 crisis. Dave 'Moral Hazard' Bahnsen delivers it.*"

—AMITY SHLAES, Board Chair, Coolidge Presidential Foundation

"*In his thought-provoking, brilliant new book, David Bahnsen brings to light, in an easy to read style, the necessary components for building and maintaining a prosperous and moral society. Personal responsibility, opportunity, and limited government are cornerstones for success for all Americans. It is a must read.*"

—SALLY PIPES, President, Pacific Research Institute

"*Bahnsen has produced the quintessential counter-narrative to both the 2008 financial collapse and the 2016 presidential election. The theme of both individual and institutional responsibility was a major driving force behind the founding of our nation, and it was a guiding principle until at least halfway through the twentieth century. Its evaporation in recent decades has dramatically altered our culture. Bahnsen exposes this crisis and shows us the way out of it. I eagerly endorse this book, but I must say that the most telling endorsement is nothing I could say, but rather the author himself, whom I have known for twenty years as the epitome of individual responsibility. This man practices what he preaches. It is principally for this reason that I urge you to listen to his preaching: the more David Bahnsens that emerge, the fewer cultural crises we would suffer.*"

—P. ANDREW SANDLIN, Founder and President,
Center for Cultural Leadership

"*Bahnsen brings rare assets to his treatment of the 2008 financial crisis. He has decades of first-hand experience in the financial industry, a keen understanding of economics, and a willingness to make fair but unpopular moral judgments. Together, these allow him to offer an account of the crisis that is both precise and comprehensive. The financial crisis is, in part, a tale of morality. But it's not the cartoon morality tale that demonizes stereotypical villains and lets the rest of us off the hook. If we want to avoid a future crisis like the last one, we need to learn the lessons Bahnsen offers.*"

—JAY RICHARDS, Senior Fellow, Discovery Institute; Professor,
Catholic University of America

CRISIS OF RESPONSIBILITY

FOREWORD BY DAVID FRENCH

CRISIS OF
RESPONSIBILITY

Our Cultural
Addiction to Blame
and How You
Can Cure It

DAVID L. BAHNSEN

A POST HILL PRESS BOOK

Crisis of Responsibility
Our Cultural Addiction to Blame and How You Can Cure It
© 2019 by David L. Bahnsen
All Rights Reserved
First Post Hill Press Hardcover Edition: February 2018

ISBN: 978-1-64293-017-7

Cover Design by Tricia Principe, principedesign.com
Interior Design and Composition by Greg Johnson/Textbook Perfect

No part of this book may be reproduced, stored in a retrieval system, or transmitted by any means without the written permission of the author and publisher.

Published in association with the literary agency of Legacy, LLC, 501 N. Orlando Avenue, Suite #313-348, Winter Park, FL 32789.

Post Hill Press
New York · Nashville
posthillpress.com

Published in the United States of America

For Joleen,
who has kept me on the path of a virtuous life
more than I deserve,
and who joined me so many years ago
on a lifetime journey where commitment and love
have been blessings, not burdens,
and where the rewards have been not just prosperous,
but the stuff dreams are made of.

CONTENTS

FOREWORD

My friend David Bahnsen's book comes to us in a time of trouble. On August 12, 2017, a Nazi-sympathizing white supremacist rammed his car into a group of leftist protesters, killing one young woman and injuring nineteen. This hideous terrorist attack occurred after a night and day of so-called "alt-right" marches through the city of Charlottesville, Virginia—marches attended by hundreds of mostly young men who held aloft torches in the night and chanted about the "blood and soil" of white nationalism.

This attack occurred not quite two months after an enraged supporter of Bernie Sanders walked onto a baseball field in Alexandria, Virginia, and opened fire on a collection of Republican congressmen who were practicing for an annual charity baseball game. It was only through good fortune and enormous personal courage that this one man didn't kill a large percentage of GOP members of the House and Senate.

The list of violent American political acts could roll on and on. Unquestionably, the nation is reaching a period of turmoil not seen since the bad days of the late 1960s and early 1970s. White supremacists have killed men in New York, Maryland, and Oregon. In Kansas, a man angry at immigrants opened fire on two people originally from India, killing one.

Left-wing violence has surged—especially violence directed against police. From Dallas to Baton Rouge to New York City, police ambushes have claimed life after life, and anti-police riots have burned parts of Charlotte, Ferguson, and Baltimore. In places as far-flung and widely separated as Vermont, California, Oregon, Washington State, and Missouri, left-wing violence and threats of left-wing violence have rocked college campuses.

It paints a bleak picture, but we've hardly begun to get bleak.

Just as it feels that political violence is on the edge of spinning out of control, millions of Americans are suffering from an astounding—and deadly—level of personal malaise. Young children are enduring skyrocketing levels of anxiety and depression, and adults are dying due to "deaths of despair" at a stunning rate.

Alcohol-related deaths are on the rise. Suicide rates are increasing. Opioid overdoses are at crisis levels. The level of self-inflicted harm is so great that for the first time in decades American life expectancy recently *dropped*. The United States is the most advanced nation in the world, with the highest level of insured citizens in its history, and the world leader in medical technology. Yet none of that has overcome the terrible power of despair.

Is anyone surprised, then, that American political culture is disrupted? The American people have increasingly rejected the elites that they blame for financial disruption and eternal, seemingly unwinnable wars. In 2016, they chose a bombastic reality TV star with zero political experience to run the most powerful nation in the history of the earth, and they rolled the dice with him at a time of increasing world instability and danger. Donald Trump defeated the very picture of establishment politics in Hillary Clinton, but *she* survived her primary only after her elite party establishment had put its thumb on the scales. Arguably, had her party's primary been as open and democratic as the GOP primary, the 2016 election would have featured an outsider Republican versus an avowed socialist Democrat.

While periods of disruption and dislocation are inevitable, they always seem to take us by surprise. The status quo seems like it will endure, until the very moment that it doesn't. And so it is with our modern challenge. We can't go back to September 10, 2001, to the last day of a long peace. We can't go back to the day before the financial crash, when countless millions of Americans thought that if they could believe in anything financial on this earth, they could at least believe in the value of their own home. Those times are gone. The question is now, to quote Christian thinker Francis Schaefer, "How should we then live?"

The answer boils down to a choice: Build or burn. Embrace the spirit of the American Revolution—the spirit that has sustained this nation since its founding—or lurch toward the French Revolution, to destructive and vicious rage at failed elites. Make no mistake, the spirit of the French Revolution is in the air. GOP voters demanded that Trump "burn it all down." Far-left rioters and all too many Black Lives Matter protesters have chosen to light literal fires in American streets. Even in the peaceful confines of social media and political debate, an "ends justifies the means" ethic has taken hold. Lies and vicious personal attacks are celebrated. Hatred of the other side trumps even regard for your own ideas. Winning justifies all manner of sins.

But that's antithetical to the ordered liberty envisioned by the founders of our country and demanded by our Constitution. Yes, our founders fought to overthrow a corrupt elite, but from the beginning they did so from within accountable institutions according to ancient rules of faith and morality. They fought to *build*, not ultimately to destroy, and they understood a core truth—"the Constitution of the United States was made only for a moral and religious people. It is wholly inadequate to the government of any other."

This is the truth that David Bahnsen understands. This is the truth he brings to life. In other words, you can slay all your political dragons, but—at the end of the day—*you* are the person most responsible for the outcome of your own life. Yes, elites fail, but we also fail ourselves, and a nation that loses its sense of personal responsibility can cycle through leaders and political parties without ever soothing its rage or healing its wounds.

In other words, there are wounds that public policy can't heal, and there are injustices that no court can correct. At the same time, however, there exists hope greater than any president can bring, and a renewal awaits that needn't depend on the competence of any politician. David's book answers that crucial question: "What now?" And the answer, truly, isn't found in our votes. It's not found in our anger. It's found when faithful men and women connect with a nation's founding cultural and spiritual core, accept the responsibilities of citizenship, and live with confidence and courage. That is the path forward, that is the answer to our national crisis, and that is the lesson of David's indispensable book.

David French

INTRODUCTION

How This Book Became a Book

September 2008—a watershed moment for our country and a watershed month for a lot of people. I am one of those people.

The financial crisis became a significant moment in my life and career for a lot of obvious reasons. I run a wealth management business engaged in managing people's money and financial affairs, a responsibility that intensifies significantly during moments of extraordinary distress. Living through the financial crisis and its attendant responsibilities with client capital, decision making, and good old-fashioned hand-holding was an intensely stressful experience for me, but also one that motivated me and provoked a strong sense of duty within.

I happened to be a managing director at one of Wall Street's largest investment banks at the time, so client anxieties comingled with company anxieties. With the very fate of the firm in question, transparency was understandably hard to come by. In addition, my wife and I had a three-year-old boy and a newborn baby girl at the time. Anxiety came from all directions—family, clients, company, and then, of course, from the actual crisis itself.

On a macro level, I am skeptical that history will record the financial crisis correctly. Many people know that Lehman Brothers, the famed Wall Street bank, went bankrupt. Many know that significant government assistance got thrown around Wall

Street in the aftermath. And many know that, somewhere in the middle of it all, a housing bubble burst. The aftermath of the crisis became immediately more newsworthy than the cause(s) of the crisis.

America entered an economic recession in the fall of 2008 that surpassed any economic contraction we have suffered since the Great Depression. More than a 50 percent drop in the stock market, higher than 10 percent unemployment, the longest and deepest contraction of gross domestic product since the Depression, and housing foreclosures or mortgage defaults that transcended anything we have ever seen—the financial crisis of 2008 had all of it and touched everyone.

I saw the crisis as the primary domestic news event of my adult lifetime. Because I was already deeply invested in it professionally and personally, I took on an intense study of the crisis in the years that followed. Even as the crisis lingered, the punditry class began analyzing and proposing various policy lessons and prescriptions. Indeed, the movement began prior to the eventual GDP recovery and the violent and shocking comeback of the stock market. From media figures to economists, financial analysts to politicians, actual stakeholders and policymakers during the crisis, a plethora of perspectives floated about in the years that followed regarding what happened, why it happened, and what it all meant.

I read every book I could get my hands on. I do not exaggerate in saying that understanding the crisis became an obsession—for two reasons. I wanted to better myself, of course, but I was also confident a revisionist narrative would eventually get baked into society's understanding of the crisis. Sadly, I was all too right.

Alongside my journey to better understand the crisis, I became sensitive to the intuitions and impulses of those around me regarding its circumstances. In social circles, I saw questionable behavior justified as a rational response to questionable behavior by other institutions enmeshed in the financial crisis. Already polarized political lines darkened considerably. What I observed validated a thesis I had, by then, developed: the financial crisis was not the cause of, but a symptom of a broader cultural *crisis of responsibility*.

The actors in this crisis were not limited to any one group. The cast in the escapade included people of all walks of life—lenders, bankers, politicians, central bankers, policymakers, and homeowners themselves. All discussions of the financial crisis turned into a blame game, with only one common thread: the target of the blame would be whatever culprit you were most conditioned to dislike in the first place—your own personal bogeyman.

I set out to write a book about the financial crisis. At that point, I fancied myself one of the most well-read people in the country on the topic, having read well over seventy books and thousands of pages of periodicals, journals, and white papers on the subject. I spent hours upon hours talking to hedge fund managers, elected officials, and other thought leaders to pick their brains. What I discovered was that I had a rather unique perspective on the crisis, one that carried not only helpful economic and historical commentary, but also a valuable lesson regarding our cultural addiction to blame.

As the years went by, I brought my wealth management business out of the aforementioned Wall Street firm (to be independent), but the impact of the financial crisis and the need for a more coherent societal lesson remained vitally important to me.

Then 2016 happened. A populist uprising took place. I don't refer only to the presidential election in the United States, but to a broader reality both here in the U.S. and abroad. At the movement's root was a deep dissatisfaction with the status quo. In the aftermath of the financial crisis, successful people had seen their balance sheets significantly restored, housing prices had recovered and then some, stock markets and bond markets were generating unprecedented returns, and the top end of the income scale was skyrocketing.

Yet culturally, things weren't quite so copasetic. Significant socioeconomic divides existed with entire segments of the U.S. population feeling abandoned and ignored. Previous years had seen a lot of concentrated angst about the crisis, but 2016 saw the catalysts to those tensions diversify. The financial crisis had not exited the stage; instead it was now joined by trade agreements, immigration challenges, government malfeasance, income inequality, student loan debt, geopolitical pacts, educational discrimination, and a plethora of other political, economic, and cultural issues driving a wedge deeper into our society.

All of it disrupted the American dream I believe in deeply. I shelved the financial crisis book, but maintained its underlying thesis. I turned my attention to evaluating the broader stressors at work in our society. My analysis of that distress—and beliefs about those issues—became the subject of this book. The motivation behind this book is the same desire I had when I set out to draft a book about the financial crisis. I offer a counter-narrative to the recent developments and significant events, and I propose a constructive path forward by which we can learn from past mistakes and create better opportunity in the future. As has been the case with the financial crisis, many events dominating the headlines today are symptoms of an entirely different problem, a deeper problem with disturbing cultural implications.

In the pages that follow, I identify that problem and suggest a path forward to a better destination—a free and virtuous society. But to get there, we must first overcome this present challenge—our cultural crisis of responsibility.

1
BUILDING WALLS
A New Era

There are more ideas on earth than intellectuals imagine. And these ideas are more active, stronger, more resistant, more passionate than politicians think. But it is because the world has ideas (and because it constantly produces them) that it is not passively ruled by those who are its leaders or those who would like to teach it, once and for all, what it must think.

—MICHEL FOUCAULT

In the case of everything that belongs to the realm of sentiment, religion, politics, morality, the affections, and antipathies, etc. The most eminent men seldom surpass the standard of the most ordinary individuals. From the intellectual point of view an abyss may exist between a great mathematician and his boot-maker, but from the point of view of character, the difference is often slight or nonexistent.

—GUSTAVE LE BON

June 23, 2016—the voters of the United Kingdom went to the ballot box to express their views on a controversial referendum to exit the European Union. Although Brexit, the shorthand term for the vote, had taken hold in American media, the substance of the referendum, and certainly the true implications, meant very little to the average American.

For one thing, the referendum was not expected to pass. Polls had fluctuated a bit, with some showing it modestly leading and some showing it modestly failing. Betting markets consistently showed the referendum likely to fail. Despite being averse to any form of uncertainty, U.S. stock markets rallied dramatically the week before the vote. Clearly, few believed something as dramatic as a world superpower (Britain) leaving a core global institution (the European Union) was likely to happen. As the Dow Jones Industrial Average advanced 500 points in the week before the vote, pundits proclaimed that cooler heads would prevail. Rational, mature voters would override the temper tantrums of the ignorant few.

I had an uncommon opinion about the vote. I was (and remain) convinced that a British exit from the European Union would be the right decision for Britain. And yet, I was also convinced it would not prevail. Polls, betting markets, and, most significantly, the ruling elites of most institutions agreed it simply would not pass, regardless of the merits of the arguments.

Yes, there was some angst among the masses to be addressed. Sure, the more liberal posture on refugee immigration had created complexities in Britain (and across Europe) that were proving to be a bit of a nuisance. But, at the end of the day, the esteemed wisdom of the elites would prevail. The people would fall in line, the elites told us. The advanced and cosmopolitan population of Britain wouldn't dare cross the wisdom of unaccountable bureaucrats in Brussels.

The elites had it all wrong.

Brexit was less about the arguments for and against and more about what the vote itself revealed. The vote revealed a paradigm shift taking place around the world that transcends the United Kingdom.

Yes, the voters of Britain stood against global authoritarianism, and, yes, they stand to benefit from reclaiming their sovereignty on matters of immigration, trade, and geopolitical policy. But the Brexit vote revealed something real and profound—a growing sense of distrust toward and dissatisfaction with the institutions of modern society. It gave voice to the growing belief that the cultural elite—long believed to be the responsible ones in society—have lost their way.

To be fair, elitist arrogance that Brexit would not pass was forgivable. Even supporters of the move, like myself, predicted failure. I appeared as the "pro-Brexit" advocate in a May 2016 debate sponsored by the World Affairs Council and British-American Business Council. My "anti-Brexit" debate opponent, former Allergan CEO David Pyott, argued passionately that the move would be a disaster to British economic opportunity. I argued in defense of Britain's sovereignty and the opportunity to enhance their economic standing outside the European Union. After two hours of debate, the moderator asked for a show of hands as to who believed the Brexit vote would pass. Almost no one raised a hand—not even me—in spite of nearly half the audience agreeing with me by the end of the evening.

Ironically, the arrogance with which elitists predicted the disintegration of British society discredited the ruling class. I appeared as a special guest on CNBC's *Squawk Box* the morning after the referendum vote to discuss the stock market outlook in light of the Brexit surprise. Stocks were indeed pointing downward that morning. *Financial Times* managing editor Gillian Tett appeared on the show just before me. She pontificated that the Brexit impact would be on the scale of the Lehman Brothers bankruptcy of 2008—the precursor to the largest financial crisis of the last eighty years!

Her prophecy of market collapse and economic catastrophe stood in stark contrast to my claims on the show minutes later.

Famed economist Jim Grant joined me to insist Brexit not only was not a systemic event, but also was likely to create incredible buying opportunities if market prices dropped enough. To be candid, neither one of us could have guessed the market drop would end in a few days. The ensuing post-Brexit market sell-off would last only forty-eight hours. Markets would fully recover and even set new highs just days after the vote.

Nevertheless, behemoth financial institutions said they would be forced to withdraw thousands of jobs from London if Brexit were approved. To date, no such job relocations have taken place, and superpower financial firms have walked back such Chicken Little forecasts. In the face of such fearmongering, the vote of the British people to exit the European Union was quite the declaration. They no longer only questioned the *legitimacy* of "the establishment"—they questioned its very *credibility*.

Trumping Brexit

Not to be left out in 2016, America also demanded a seat at the table of unexpected political transformation. The contrarian reality of the Donald J. Trump candidacy and eventual election to the presidency made Brexit look like a sideshow. Campaigning as a sort of conservative Huey Long, the billionaire real estate developer and Fifth Avenue Manhattan resident ran the first populist campaign since Ross Perot—and the first successful one in a century or more.

Initially dismissed as a publicity-seeking reality TV star (including by this author), his campaign quickly morphed into one of the most historical political events of our lifetimes. His road to the Republican nomination first had to go through some of the most qualified and recognizable Republican candidates ever assembled. From the extremely well-financed, former successful governor of Florida, Jeb Bush, to the young conservative stars Marco Rubio and Ted Cruz, each member of the sixteen-person field tried and failed to block the nomination of Donald Trump. The candidates were not considered weak conservatives or questionable Republicans. They were mostly traditional Reaganite conservatives, strong on Republican orthodoxy and untainted by scandal or personal damage to their candidacies. But in 2016, traditional Republican orthodoxies weren't generating massive crowds or blowout primary wins. The broad policy platform that has always served the Republican Party well—tax cuts, smaller government, balanced budgets, entitlement reform, and the hope of a more restrained Supreme Court—were not enough. In fact, they were not even necessary.

A sort of poetry took over the 2016 election cycle. It was decidedly sociological, populist in nature, and struck a unique chord in the national psyche. Time and time again, enthusiasts for Donald Trump claimed they were attracted by his "outsider" status and commitment to change the way business is done in Washington, DC. Trump complained about Wall Street; the business-friendly GOP base ate it up. He criticized the Left, not for being too liberal but for being ineffective. He didn't campaign on making government smaller; he campaigned on making it more productive (more "businesslike"). He didn't try that hard to reach out to the social conservative wing of the Republican party; he reached out to all in the party who were tired of media bias and political correctness. He donned a red ball cap and filled arenas with thousands of people as he promised to undo the damage caused by the "establishment"—lumping the media, the Beltway insiders, and the GOP leadership all under one broad tent.

A fair and charitable interpretation of the Trump movement, and certainly of his successful bid for the presidency, is that Trump was an imperfect candidate who crafted the perfect message for a key constituency—a certain middle-class and lower middle-class economic group that had not participated in the economic growth of the last two decades.

The message was simple: the system had been rigged against them. Regardless of the messenger, that message resonated. From free trade deals such as the North American Free Trade Agreement (NAFTA) and the proposed Trans-Pacific Partnership (TPP), to the rising number of immigrants who crossed our southern border illegally, to the war in Iraq which cost unfathomable dollars without a clear win for America, to the way China managed its currency, to American companies sending jobs offshore—Donald Trump tapped into a list of frustrations.

Most importantly, all of them provided reasons for this frustrated and neglected constituency to feel like victims. All of them provided bogeymen, problems that President Trump promised to confront and resolve. All of them fed a powerful narrative that establishment forces had enjoyed their fun for far too long. A new sheriff was coming to town.

This political phenomenon would never have happened if this target voting market hadn't been frustrated to begin with. Although the phenomenon hit its peak in 2016, resulting in the nomination and eventual election of Donald Trump, the reality is that it had been building for at least an election cycle or two before it. Rick Santorum, a perfect encapsulation of social conservatism and economic populism, came extremely close to winning the Republican nomination in 2012. In the cycle before that, Mike Huckabee, an early representation of that same blend, was the near spoiler. While neither Santorum nor Huckabee crossed the finish line, their unlikely and extraordinary showings demonstrated that populist angst was brewing.

Many perspectives exist about each of the 2016 campaign issues, and, indeed, this book will parse some of those issues with what I hope to be precision and fairness. But like the Brexit vote, the media and punditry class simply could not believe what they were seeing take place. I'm not referring merely to those who didn't believe Donald Trump would prevail in the race (that included the vast majority of Americans). I'm referring to those who could not see the movement, did not understand the pent-up generational resentment, and were not convinced any cultural divide existed in the first place.

The 2016 Trump win revealed that a large segment of the country had no clue what an even larger segment of the country felt. As with the Brexit tale, myopia was most prevalent in large cities, coastal enclaves, and the big media and financial firms. Sociological disparity more than partisan differences caused them to miss the reality that a significant bloc of Americans felt left behind.

Understanding that angst, the reasons for it, and the cultural implications of it on our economy is the subject of this book. I don't intend to address the question of whether or not Donald Trump represents the solution to specific campaign issues. At the time of this writing, he is the president of the United States. In due time there will be a political and historical record of his presidency and the impact of his policies. That is not my aim here.

I want to go deeper, into the cultural substrata, to discover what has gone wrong for so many in this new era of the American experiment. I'll candidly consider the implications of what we find and identify the chief malady keeping us from confronting what I call a crisis of responsibility—our cultural addiction to blame.

Someone Blame Somebody for Something

I focus on economics, not only because of my financial expertise, but because economics matter a great deal in assessing the lay of the land. Since the U.S. financial crisis of 2008, GDP growth has underperformed its own trend growth by at least 1 percent per year (see Fig. 1.1).[1] As a result, our economy is estimated to be $2.8 trillion less than it otherwise should be.

A series of cultural and economic factors contributed to this break from trend line growth, creating a negative feedback loop. Consequently, the growth disruption itself has exacerbated the cultural and economic malignance that helped create the underperforming trend in the first place. Serious analysts must be careful not to miss the vicious, cyclical nature of this effect.

However, the angst-filled population bloc that revolted against globalism and institutionalism of all stripes is probably not parsing distinctions about GDP growth, economic causation, and other such academic nuance. Hundreds of millions of people worldwide have simply lost faith in the "smartest people in the room," the alleged gatekeepers of the economy, key institutions,

FIGURE 1.1

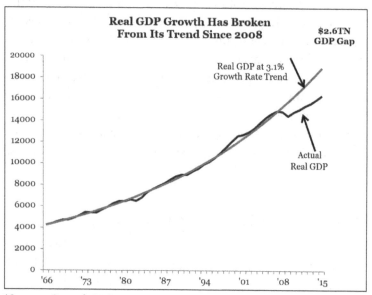

Strategas Research, 2017

and political structures in society. Much of their lack of confidence is wholly justified, even if the frustrated don't fully understand what has caused the problem.

But they want someone to blame for it. As I'll demonstrate throughout the book, what has emerged in our culture is a "scapegoatism" run amok—a victim mentality that is dangerous to all, regardless of political affinity or socioeconomic class.

Our stalling GDP growth didn't cause the current unrest, although it has accelerated it. Many other economic data points enter the fray, but the break from trend line growth captures nearly all of them. Wage growth has continued to stagnate. The income inequality conversation seems to have transcended normal class-warfare rhetoric. While many of the economic forces behind the present era are abstruse, a paycheck that isn't growing is simple to understand. Human nature being human nature, people watching their paychecks decline tend to become resentful toward those experiencing income growth. Trade deficits are not easy to comprehend (quite frankly, as I'll demonstrate in later chapters, even many professional economists do not understand trade deficits), but the general feeling is that most people are now on the outside looking in at the real opportunities.

One need not be a neo-Marxian or class-warfare leftist to see that the green-eyed monster of economic envy has been stirring for years and laid the foundation for many of the walls—ideological, social, and physical—that we hear so much about in this new, angst-driven era.

This new era is not defined solely by an economic and political tantrum. A significant number of Americans feel talked down to, forgotten, and disconnected. Blue-collar whites don't feel only economically separated from white-collar whites, but socially separated, as well. Political analyst Sean Trende refers to this divide as "cultural cosmopolitanism" versus "cultural traditionalism."[2] These two camps have different perspectives on family, church, education, and country. Their cultural differences have produced a level of social angst, because the more cosmopolitan camp largely "occupies the commanding heights of American culture."[3] The result is a complete distrust of key institutions in our society. The media, big business, big finance, and higher education are now often held in contempt, not just for their ideology (though that's part of it), but because they collectively form someone to blame for the present malaise—a composite scapegoat, if you will, on which fears can be placed and railed against at rallies.

Are the fears fair and coherent? Certainly not. But they're not irrational and random either. As my colleague Jonah Goldberg, leading conservative pundit at the National Review Institute, says:

> To the extent that Donald Trump has damaged democratic norms, his success is attributable to the fact that elites—in journalism, but also in academia and elsewhere—have corrupted those norms to the point where a lot of people see them as convenient tools for only one side in the political and cultural wars of our age.[4]

Thus, my objective in the pages that follow is to sort the truth from the misunderstandings about what has compromised American productivity and, indeed, American prosperity. It is not my intent to defend the forces of anti-elitism or anti-globalism, which have so much momentum in this new era. In fact, my intent is to provoke a counterintuitive conversation about what really ails us all, and offer concrete suggestions as to where substantive and generational remedies may be found—if we have the courage and candor to pursue them.

I don't intend merely to condemn one guilty party (arrogant institutional elites), but then embrace an ignorant victim mentality that ignores the cultural tides of this era. The paradigm for returning to the possibility of prosperity for all is not one of choosing between the elites and non-elites, the strong and the weak, or the influential and the oppressed. That's the picture that *has* been painted. It is not lacking some prima facie support, but it is incomplete at best, and dangerous at worst.

My counterintuitive presupposition is that the forces of elitism and statism, which are so despised by so many, stand to grow by leaps and bounds as a result of this present global angst, *if* we fail to understand the core cause. If the efforts to delegitimize and disempower elite forces is temporarily successful, but the weak and morally emasculated alternative falls on its face, I am quite convinced that out of the ashes of this groundswell failure will come greater bureaucracy, greater institutional arrogance, and far-reaching top-down authoritarianism that will crush the cause of freedom.

There is no wall in this new era that cleanly divides us into two sides. One may advocate for free trade and still support Brexit (as this author does). One may live in a more culturally cosmopolitan part of society and still be patriotic to the core. On the myriad of issues in our national conversation, there is room for nuance in almost every single one. A sincere investigation of these issues will not create a simple, binary choice between "establishment" and "populists."

And yet, the one perspective that has the potential to destroy us all, and which must be unilaterally rejected if we are to stave off the coming authoritarian backlash, is embracing victimhood. To reject victimhood, we must first understand *how* and *why* so many hot-button issues are being framed as scapegoat issues, reasons for someone to blame somebody for something.

Room exists for disagreement on policy specifics on issues like immigration and trade, but there can be no doubt about these three things:

1. A new era is upon us, and the political, social, economic, and cultural effects are just beginning.
2. Our path forward must reject the institutional arrogance and elitism of top-down control.
3. Yet, we must recognize our cultural addiction to blame, properly understand the key issues, and forge a new culture of responsibility in which free people become virtuous people, and virtuous people become productive people.

Where It All Begins

There exists a tension in these present times for people of my ideological bent. That tension partly motivates my writing. On one hand, there are natural forces in society right now that demand attention. The beliefs that created a large and impotent European Union are real. A form of secular humanism has clearly metastasized in our culture, aided by the ivory tower of academia and the liberal, unchecked media. The economic landscape has helped create a frustrated group of people who feel forgotten and alienated. Those who resent the arrogance of elitists are not without basis; those who portray economic frustration are not fabricating these sensations from thin air.

These are all true; however, what is "on the other hand" is what drives my passion on these pages. There is no need to ignore the reasons for angst, but we do need to get the remedy right. Any prescription that misidentifies either the cause or the cure could prove fatal for the patient.

I am a limited-government advocate who has long believed that the size of government is in direct, inverse correlation to the responsibility of the people. My concern is that behind much of the cultural angst today is a narrative that blames great and powerful forces, not unlike the mysterious, unknowable wizard behind the screen in Oz. These forces become the scapegoats, almost always with some level of legitimacy, while individual people are indemnified.

I contend that the key stakeholders in our societies—individuals, families, and communities—must not be permitted to play victim and avoid careful scrutiny. Where policies and prevailing attitudes have served to disenfranchise some, we must note it as such and fight for change. Yet where irresponsibility abounds and culpability lies, we must say so and prescribe solutions that honor the dignity of every stakeholder while calling them to greater moral accountability and individual responsibility.

Trade, immigration, capital markets, big media, and other global realities are key issues to be addressed. However, the key to American prosperity is not to feed our cultural addiction to blame, but to begin—right here, with both you and me—to make responsibility matter again.

2

NAME YOUR BOGEYMAN

Wall Street, Washington, NAFTA, China, Mexico, and the Media

The fault, dear Brutus, is not in our stars, but in ourselves.

—CASSIUS

Whose fault is it? Who is to blame for today's plight of the alleged common man? Have institutions, countries, policies, and traditions suffocated the middle class, or have these dastardly bogeymen been exaggerated, or even fabricated, to provide cover for the sins of the middle class?

In the chapters that follow, I'll dive deeper into an examination of the most popular bogeymen offered of late, but are more nuances needed to correctly assign blame? Furthermore, do each of these forces need to be evaluated individually, or are they all part of a monolithic driver that is deteriorating quality of life and opportunity for middle America while promoting the interests of the global elite?

My research and commitment to basic integrity suggests that only an individual analysis of each bogeyman will provide the appropriate optics and ability to form cogent conclusions.

Are there overlaps and collusions (for example, between corporate America and the "K Street" lobbyists of Washington, DC)? Sure! But will it be fairer and more appropriate to look at each bogeyman candidate on a case-by-case basis? I believe so.

Why does it matter—the "one" versus the "many" approach? Why is it critical that we consider the issue—the collective bogeymen versus the choice of an individual? For one thing, the rise of the single, collective bogeyman—a composite of popular societal demons—is a reasonably new phenomenon. Angst against Wall Street is most definitely nothing new; however, a shared distrust of *both* Wall Street *and* free trade *is* new. In the 1980s, we heard whispered concerns about a Japan-centric global economic movement, so we aspired to greater integration with Mexico. Today, Mexican immigration is considered a blight for American workers. Cheaper goods entering the American economy from China is considered to be another. In fact, cheap labor from the south *and* cheap products from the east are both said to be damaging American jobs.

One of the amazing things about the Trump campaign was how it tapped into a new and reasonably undefined angst that lumped nearly every major institution into one aggregate bogeyman (big business, big finance, big government, big media, big trade, big global growth, etc.). His campaign resonated with a society ready to blame this composite bogeyman for the problems they faced and felt.

How did these entities come to be viewed collectively rather than individually? It was inevitable. When one seeks to cast blame, it is only a matter of time until a multitude of candidates surface, each with some level of plausible culpability. To make an open-and-shut case against any one candidate is difficult, but making a rhetorically loose case against *all* the candidates together can seem weighty and quite compelling. And it certainly can be emotionally gratifying. The frustration only needed to build to critical mass.

It was probably the 2008 financial crisis that first offered this collective bogeyman by offering a hodgepodge of culprits as the objects of middle-class frustration. The Right was all too happy to blame either the Federal Reserve for reckless monetary policy or Washington, DC, housing policy for irresponsible lending. The Left didn't have to stray far from long-held conventions to fault Wall Street's cavalier greed and leverage. The consequences from the financial crisis of 2008—the deepest recession since the Great Depression, a 50 percent drop in the overinflated prices of residential real estate, a stock market collapse, and double-digit unemployment—were so severe and unavoidable that any post-crisis download was bound to forge strange alliances.

I'll attempt to sort the fair from the preposterous in chapter 4 as to what exactly *did* happen in the financial crisis, but my point here is that those events accelerated the formation of this new, composite bogeyman. Factor in several postcrisis years of muted economic growth, the immigration side effects plaguing much of Europe, and then the popularity and media-savvy style of a long-time economic nationalist in Donald Trump,[5] and it's easy to see how Wall Street, free trade, big business, the press, and China all ended up inside the bull's-eye. Each of these may have taken decades to develop as a viable target, but they all aligned in recent years to create such a perception of a united effect that those who feel aggrieved now see little distinction between them.

The challenge in the chapters ahead is to recognize the sometimes troubling social, economic, and cultural consequences of these various forces, while avoiding superficially simple conclusions—*if* and *when* simple explanations are inadequate. Each of the bogeymen du jour has problems, and each has contributed to the plight of working-class America; nevertheless, neither none nor all, taken individually or collectively, can tell the whole story of where we are and why.

Most importantly, they cannot reveal what it will take to make America great again. Consequently, in the pages that follow, I will offer neither vindication nor immunity to any of them, nor will I try to craft or endorse a single, consensus view about them. I believe the true culprit we must fear lies deeper, closer to our cultural heart and soul.

Wall Street: Case in Point

Our discussion of Wall Street, for example, will focus on the financial crisis and provide a framework for evaluating so many of these bogeymen. Wall Street is a *creature of*, not the *cause of*, what plagues the culture. The mere existence of sophisticated capital markets in America is not a negative; it is actually a *sine qua non* in the American economy. Furthermore, hating Wall Street is nothing new. It has invited public scorn since the beginning of modern finance, because class envy sells, because arrogance and indifference has often emanated from the pillars of finance, and because it is so easy for press and politician alike to tap into class frustrations.

However, the job growth made possible by sophisticated capital markets is undeniable. A financed and capitalized post–Industrial Revolution America brought tens of millions of people into a decent wage and quality of life. It is a historical fact. Life in America would be unimaginably worse if we banned deal making, trading, advising, structuring, and synergizing the capital structure of American business. Must capital markets in our country be accompanied by systemic risk, brute arrogance, and excessive greed? Certainly not! But we do need capital markets, even though cultural and moral deficiencies in society, a permeation of poor business ethics, may be magnified in the world of finance. Such is the nature of things—the power and material prosperity involved in directing capital markets is highly susceptible to excess.

When I entered my career in financial services, I was certainly affected by the Hollywood characterization of Wall Street as a place of hedonistic greed and excess. Whether I liked it or believed it, I had a vision of Manhattan skyscrapers filled with Gordon Gekko–like characters from the 1987 movie *Wall Street.* I pictured buildings full of wealthy men who cut deals all day and partied all night—people who lied, cheated, and stole from one another, then attended $1,000/plate black-tie galas alongside accomplices and victims. It didn't take me long to realize that a movie made about what really happens on Wall Street would disappoint ticket buyers immensely.

As in any business, there are, of course, bad apples. Certainly, some folks live on the edge of hedonistic pleasure (an indictment hardly unique to Wall Street, and far more prevalent on college campuses than in the corridors of American finance). I found very few Gordon Gekkos and quite a few soccer dads. There are men and women with tremendous career aspirations (hardly a sin), but the vast majority of people I've worked with on Wall Street, from senior leadership positions at behemoth investment banks, to top hedge fund managers, to bond and equity traders across Wall Street trading desks, are, well—family people. The top levels of Wall Street, the middle management of American banks, and the exciting throes of traders and asset managers are all people who put pants on one leg at a time. Like so many in middle-class America, they're often hopeful about their annual bonus, stressed about their kids' grades, and almost always patriotic. In other words, they are generally *normal* people.

Wall Street is truly a challenging force to either attack or defend. For one thing, it's hard to define. It is not a physical place anymore. Wall Street's geographical diversification accelerated since 9/11, but it was in motion prior to that day for a number of reasons. First, finance had become globalized (Deutsche Bank, UBS, Barclays, and others are all "Wall Street" firms—meaning global financial superpowers—but they're all based in Europe). Second, even within Manhattan, New York–based firms have diversified all over the metropolitan area (from midtown to Lower Manhattan to Hudson Yards). Third, with the advent of Silicon Valley forty years ago, venture capital firms became an increasingly potent part of capital markets, making the west coast (San Francisco, Menlo Park, Palo Alto) every bit as relevant of a cultural finance center as New York.

Consequently, when we use the term "Wall Street" now, we don't refer to the iconic street that runs from the East River to Broadway in Lower Manhattan, off of which the New York Stock Exchange sits, mere blocks from where the Twin Towers once stood tall. Rather, Wall Street is a catchall phrase for modern financial institutions, from the behemoth private equity name Blackstone in midtown Manhattan, to the often vilified Goldman Sachs in Lower Manhattan, to the British behemoth Barclays across the pond, to the venture capital genius of Kleiner Perkins in Menlo Park. Why does it matter? The lack of specificity about what Wall Street is, and *what* or *who* one is referring to when decrying "Wall Street," has greatly helped the cause of her critics.

Not coincidentally, the same is true regarding criticisms of free trade and Washington, DC. The tighter and more specific the enemy becomes, the greater the burden to justify accusations, connect dots, and present the case for real, definable iniquity from very specific actors. That is not to say it can't be done. There is plenty of opportunity to find real malfeasance from real people when discussing Wall Street or Washington. However, we are talking about a broader cultural narrative that has taken hold, and narratives do not like specifics. A broader lambasting of an entire institution is easier, as it plays into the human tendency for scapegoating. Plus, it provides psychological comfort for people to believe some (or all) woes are the by-product of a massive, undefeatable force.

If one were to say, *Bill stole from me,* evidence would be required. There would need to be specific scrutiny of Bill, a real and narrow fact pattern, and, at the end of the day, a conclusion about what *exactly* Bill did or did not do. But if one says, *Wall Street is ripping us off*—then all such specifics get bypassed. *Us* is usually a consortium of middle-class, working people who don't take car services to work or vacation in the Hamptons. The imagery alone promotes an "us versus them" binary scenario where generalizations can be accepted without much discrimination whatsoever. Accepting as fact that large, undefined entities are working against you is the mother of fatalism. Several beliefs and conclusions slide down the slippery slope from that fatalistic presupposition and serve a dual purpose. They muddy the waters of self-evaluation and numb the responsibility sensors of the people who choose to see themselves as victims.

As I'll reveal in chapter 4, the financial crisis allowed a broad narrative to form that vindicated many guilty people—individuals walking away from the responsibility of making a house payment they were often completely capable of making, for example. The narrative also condemned many entities without justification, such as those who provided capital to people who would later walk away from what they owed. As I'll demonstrate, the financial leverage and greed that nearly brought down many financial superpowers was cut from the same cloth as the financial leverage and greed that became systemic across all of society. In other words, Wall Street was no innocent party in the financial crisis, but their greedy actions were within the same negative feedback loop as the rest of society—short sightedness, myopia, buck passing, and total disregard for how one's actions may affect others.

The immoral climate ran deep and wide. It did not exclude Wall Street, by any means, but it didn't begin there either. It was part of a vicious cycle created by a cultural decline of thoughtful interconnected consideration, morality, integrity, and personal responsibility.

Like each of the popular bogeymen, Wall Street has a core function that is not only good, but vital. Like all the others, it features excesses and cringe-worthy examples of selfishness, but as long as we have capitalism, we will have capital markets. Lovers of liberty and freedom should want vibrant capital markets driving free and open markets of business and innovation. Wall Street's vital function—providing capital for American business to grow, innovate, fund expansion, and globally compete—should not be demonized. And yet, where policies do help the privileged few *at the expense of* the struggling many, we do have a duty to resist and seek change. The ability to match investors and lenders with projects and entrepreneurs is true and indisputable, *and* there should be no justification for greed, fraud, distortion, corruption, or excess.

In chapter 6, I'll dissect crony capitalism and the insidious effects that corruption and special favors create in a market economy. But I conclude these prefatory thoughts on Wall Street by making one thing clear: *my defense of capital markets in no way defends crony capitalism.* Quite the contrary, crony corruption jeopardizes the very aim of free markets. The net positive effects of Wall Street—matching buyers and sellers, aligning investors and projects, and advising on the most rational use of capital— are diluted when public confidence disintegrates as a result of special treatment or outright fraud.

Unfortunately, the angst in this new era has failed to delineate between healthy, competitive markets and suspect cronyism. Restoring American prosperity will require not only robust capital markets, which we surely have, but also an American people who believe the financiers are not out to get them. Reacquiring that belief will require an end to the scapegoating, significant reform within Wall Street, proper alignment of incentives, and a societal re-moralization that brings Wall Street along with it.

Even Stranger Bedfellows

These same principles can and must be applied to the other popular targets of cultural frustration. Washington, DC, is perhaps the hardest to defend, for there is a significant challenge inherent in the very concept of political power. From the days of a king in ancient times, we know of the propensity for political power to corrupt, to cater to special interests, and to serve the needs of the few and privileged at the expense of the many. But even a rather logical bogeyman candidate like government requires some specificity, doesn't it?

Is Washington hurting everyday Americans because it is doing too much, or because it is doing too little? Don't we often hear *both* claims? Can they both be true? Is Washington, DC, doing the little guy wrong because DC is big, powerful, and effective at squashing the little guy while coordinating with special interests? Or is DC hurting the little guy because Washington is weak, inefficient, bureaucratic, disorganized, and mostly inept? We need specifics to discern the answers.

I'll be the first to confess, it would be easier to defend Wall Street than to defend big government. Neither Congress nor the federal executive branch bureaucracy has given much defense-worthy material to use against the charge of complete ineffectiveness. However, the narrative in this new era seems to be that too much government has done too much harm to too many people. So one can see why it is both confusing and dangerous to suggest that the antidote would be more government doing more for even more people. Government perhaps most clearly deserves to be on the bogeyman list, but it should be placed there for rational and intelligent reasons, not for mere rhetorical convenience.

The truth about the complexity of today's angst is this: *there is no consensus amongst those who claim to be aggrieved by government as to what the grievance is.* That's another reason why deciding if we are angry because government has tried to do too much or too little is not insignificant. For now, everyone seems willing for both camps to coexist. Indeed, the Trump coalition consisted of both small-government libertarian types who believe government has exceeded its natural role and constitutional place, and those who believe their plight can be resolved by government. These two incompatible viewpoints allied to help Trump win. The incompatibility may not have been deeply questioned in the 2016 election cycle, but how the relationship between government and citizenry is defined in the years to come will be, perhaps, the pivotal public issue that determines the direction of American prosperity.

It does not make things simpler to acknowledge that all categories of government angst can be justified at times. Surely, we can argue that government has sometimes done too little, sometimes (most times) taken on too much (the failure of the national welfare state being a prime example), and often been inefficient and incompetent.

As a general rule, regardless of reality, people will usually pick the one box that best fits their worldview. If your natural inclination is to believe government should be doing more, you can find case after case for bemoaning too little government action—more federal funding for education, more prosecutions of Wall Street executives, more regulation of energy companies, more money toward AIDS research, and so forth. Those in this camp are usually pretty consistent: if there is a need, that need can most likely be remedied through more government action.

On the other hand, there is another camp that consistently echoes the classic joke from President Ronald Reagan: "The nine most terrifying words in the English language are, 'I'm from the government and I'm here to help.'" For this group, the size of government, not efficiency, is the problem. Government is not only failing in what it is doing; it's trying to do too much.

One of the most amazing political achievements of the Trump revolution is how he appealed to both camps despite their totally antithetical views. A large constituency of Tea Party types who would be naturally attracted to politicians like Ted Cruz supported Donald Trump because of their hostility toward big government. At the same time, a unique and unprecedented camp that was generally more prone to support the socialist Bernie Sanders also supported Donald Trump.

But the strangeness of these two bedfellows of small government versus big government polarizations paled in comparison to the unusual nature of the *technocrat* camp that supported Trump, believing he will get it done *better*. For this group, what plagues society is not insufficiently sized government (up *or* down) but an intellectually and professionally deficient government that needs someone with business acumen to run it. Put someone in charge with a track record of success and competent deal making, their thinking goes, and life will improve. Health care is not a mess because government has taken on too much or too little, but rather because they messed up whatever role they did take. Politicians are not losers because they are power hungry, or because they are inadequately competent, but rather because they are *politicians*. Their intrinsic inferiority comes from the fact that they are bureaucratic, wasteful, inefficient, and poorly prepared for the task of "getting things done."

The separation between these three camps in evaluating government is as old as the civil magistrate itself, but what is unique in modern times is the willingness of these three camps to fly together on the same political plane. Their shared anger toward the government brings them together, and the reasons for the anger, not to mention the solutions, matter not. It is a truly unique development in political history.

Once again, however, the challenge before us is to discover where the bogeyman label belongs and where it does not. The great failure of the European experiment over the last few decades has been an obese government. Lord Acton taught us that overly ambitious, centralized power has no chance of ending well. Modern Europe is the greatest nonviolent case study of this truth in history. In America, we view government *size* as one problem and *inefficiency* as another, because we fail to recognize that one (size) inevitably leads to another (inefficiency). But we also fail to realize that government grows not because of usurpation, but rather societal transfer—common apathy and popular complacence. Our system of government truly is *by the people, for the people.* Consequently, the reason big and small government critics can link arms and attack government as a bogeyman is that the government truly is a reflection of the people. (Chapter 10 elaborates on this very point.)

A representative form of government allows for very few exceptions to this statement of fact. Our government is a reflection of our people. Social ills are eating away the foundation of our society. Those social ills have created a societal vacuum that begs government to step in. The remarkable Yuval Levin argues in his masterful work *The Fractured Republic* that a big-government model has come about as a result of the ignoring and even rejecting of society's major intermediating institutions (family, community, church, social organizations, unions, fraternal organizations, etc.).

Is it possible that we have both a problem of big government *and* a problem of inefficient and inept government—*and we have brought those problems upon ourselves*? Have we, the people, handed more control of our lives and futures over to government as we have rejected social accountability and personal responsibility?

I encourage all visitors to Washington, DC, to visit the Washington Monument. It is a beautiful building with incredible history and architecture. At the top of the monument, however, one can take in breathtaking views of Washington and the Potomac alongside pictures of what that same view looked like at different stages of history. To the north, south, east, and west, one can see government buildings and departments gradually expanding over time. Needless to say, there are no iterations in which the size of government shrinks. The inevitable growth of government is powerfully, though unintentionally, captured atop the Washington Monument.

Unfortunately, this incremental growth of government is in direct inverse proportion to the responsibility of the American people. Thus our investigation into the government as scapegoat for what ails us must consider where that growth of government is doing harm, where it can be curtailed, and where government activity can simply be improved. Most people are very comfortable saying taxes are too high; very few are comfortable saying precisely what spending should be cut. I believe both taxes and spending are too high for a right-sized government, but do we have a morally capable society ready to share the burden—and opportunity—of a smaller government? (In chapters 11 and 12, I'll explain how we can reinterpret government through improved financial and cultural remedies.)

What We Need Most

China, Mexico, and trade get lumped in with the targets of the day, as well. Make no mistake: we must decipher the real ramifications to the challenges of trade, technology, automation, and globalization. I argue that trade has been a net positive to our economy, the American consumer, and society at large, and yet we must acknowledge that global trade has produced some creative destruction. Those holding out "unfair trade agreements" as their bogeyman of choice have a responsibility to consider the big economic picture, and those defending market forces of trade and technology have a responsibility to consider the downstream consequences of these evolutions.

The data will show that we face real challenges in the present context, and that those challenges have solutions and remedies available to address them. As we address these issues, we must not panic and pretend that we can stop trading with global customers and partners. That's simply not a credible option. Yet we can look beyond the bogeyman of trade and globalization and find a far more sensible economic solution than protectionism or isolationism, and a cultural antidote that is far more promising and productive.

Similarly, the media is another bogeyman that will not emerge from this discussion either with immunity or the label of culprit in chief. The Right is correct to lament the liberalization of the press and their extraordinary efforts to promote an agenda rather than report the news. However, is the press in American culture in such a tragic state because the media has made it so, or because the media is reflecting a tragic culture? Is the media the cause of an epidemic or a symptom? And are the accusations as bad as they may seem? Hasn't the internet, cable news, social media, and other modern conventions democratized the distribution of reporting and news content? Are both sides guilty to some degree of agenda-driven propaganda versus objectively reporting the news? And, most relevant to this discussion, amidst all the angst over media bias and agendas, can people really claim that a biased press has actually made their lives worse?

Once again, what we see with the media bogeyman is that the context of the accusation is truthful and accurate—unfair reporting and egregious arrogance—but with nuances that fail to identify cause and effect or eliminate individual responsibility. The media fits the narrative of a composite bogeyman advancing the needs of the global elite and powerful, but that narrative fails to explain how media shenanigans have alleviated personal responsibility.

Let's face it. It feels good to pummel a composite bogeyman. Yet the practical benefits are few. This book will fail if it merely bolsters arguments for ganging up on popular enemies of the day; nevertheless, it will also fail if it does not acknowledge the prima facie basis for angst with Wall Street, Washington, DC, foreign competitors, and others. Thus, I will examine each of these bogeymen and others in the chapters that follow. We must understand the challenges they represent and the reasons each entered the fray, but reject the notion that the need of the hour is more scapegoating. We must seek to find not excuses for what ails us, but cures that will heal us. Broad and poorly defined bogeymen will not restore American prosperity in this new era.

Finance, government, media, trade—all have a role to play, but what we need now is to end our addiction to blame and accept the responsibility that comes from being part of a society governed of, by, and for *we, the people*.

3

DISINTEGRATING RESPONSIBILITY

The Social Foreshadowing
to the Present Crisis

*To suppose that any form of government will secure liberty or
happiness without any virtue in the people is a chimerical idea.*

—JAMES MADISON

If 2016 was the year politics revealed the percolating cultural
tensions of a new global economy, then perhaps 2012 was the
year that those who believe "culture is upstream from politics"
knew it was coming.

Charles Murray's landmark book, *Coming Apart: The State of
White America, 1960–2010*, was released in 2012 to much deserved
acclaim. A political scientist and sociologist with a doctorate
from MIT and an undergraduate degree from Harvard University, Dr. Murray examined changes in American culture in the
generation that had matured since the 1960s. He purposely iso-
lated his analysis only to sociological data of white America, so
as to avoid any accusation of racial bias or affectation. The study
provided empirical data and thoughtful conclusions that were
powerful and profoundly important for those seeking to better
understand an increasingly divided culture.

The cultural context Murray described became the raw material for the political transformation of 2016. He portrayed a deeply divided and polarized white America at risk of "coming apart" further if the root cultural issues were unaddressed. Political commentary in 2016 often described the forces Trump tapped into as novel or new, but in reality, 2016 was more about politics catching up to culture. The forces of frustration had been stirring beneath the surface for quite some time.

As with many of the issues we'll examine, the consensus diagnosis that Main Street was rightly frustrated for having been victimized by some other impersonal force or societal institution doesn't completely line up with reality. The narrative many on the Right prefer is an easy one to grasp: America is a God-fearing nation filled with men and women of industry, family, and faith. The leftist forces of redistributionism, statism, humanism, and elitism have distorted, if not ruined, the righteous efforts of this core American nucleus.

I find this narrative easy to believe for it facilitates two ideas that are easier to accept than the actual truth of the matter: (1) at its core, Americana remains industrious, virtuous, and engaged; and (2) the bad guy is some chosen *-ism* closely correlated with elitism (secular academia, biased media, a liberal political establishment, and so on). In this story, hope is always right around the corner, for all we need do is to vanquish the leftism polluting the goodness of the American psyche and the righteous, industrious class will eagerly usher in the city on a hill. As this story goes, the free and virtuous society is hindered, not by the rank and file but by the culturally leftist elites who have thoroughly poisoned our institutions.

This narrative of American life is at the heart of the commercial success of conservative talk radio and many of the different expressions of right-wing media (internet, social media, cable news, and so forth). It has a clear protagonist—millions of American men and women who simply want to love God and country and take responsibility for their own economic well-being. It has a clear antagonist—leftists opposed to America's foundations who seek to reshape our country into a secular, humanistic, European welfare state.

The Unraveling of Virtue

Let's start with the parts of this narrative that are painfully true, if only incompletely so. There are elitist forces within education, the media, and the government who disdain the principles undergirding the American experiment. This fact is as obvious in modern America as any sociopolitical truism could be. For many on the Right, the efforts of the cultural Left to suppress religious liberty, to invite humanism into all aspects of the pop culture, and to redefine the story of America is a form of "civil war."[6] Indeed, this author is the first to acknowledge that the nation we wish to preserve must be protected from the immoral and anti-intellectual parasites that live off America's cultural heritage while, at the same time, trying to disconnect her from that heritage in which she can best thrive.

These leftist threats to the American project are real and often concentrated in bicoastal capitals of snobbery and anti-Western sentiment. Any comprehensive audit of the institutional forces in our society would reinforce the belief by those on the Right that elitists are actively trying to change how we live and think.

But believing that there are external forces (external to the core American nucleus of working-class folks who value God and country) accelerating our cultural and even economic demise is not the same as agreeing that those forces are the primary cause. Indeed, as Murray's book so ardently demonstrated, the cultural deterioration we see today started when the social fabric of what was once a virtuous working class began to unravel. The true story of our "coming apart" is this: rather than being the *result* of globalization and other contemporary challenges, the unraveling of virtue within the working class is actually the *root cause of our inability to properly respond.*

Murray uses the following four categories, or "founding virtues" as he calls them, to illustrate the divide between those in the higher social and economic strata of American life and those in the middle and lower segments: industriousness, honesty, marriage, and religion. Murray demonstrates using carefully analyzed data that divorce rates have come down in more affluent cities and counties. Out-of-wedlock births are also extremely rare in those places. A happy marriage, as can best be demonstrated by data from self-reporting assessments, is a more prized commodity in those communities perceived as thriving economically. These communities are often vilified as being the "winners" or "inside players" in the present global economic transformation.

The view of virtue in "blue-collar America" isn't quite as rosy. Marriage often creates and protects economic stability. It's a nearly indisputable fact. That's what's so troubling about the basic decline in the percentage of people who are married or ever have been married in our society. While over 85 percent of thirty- to forty-nine-year-old males in upper-class America are married, that number has plummeted in middle America—from 85 percent one generation ago to below 50 percent today.[7] As the chart below demonstrates (Fig. 3.1), the total percentage of married adult men has dropped from 70 percent in 1960 to only 50 percent in 2016. The percentage of never-married men has risen from 25 percent to nearly 40 percent.

All the data reinforces a basic theme: the cultural fibers in middle America haven't merely weakened over the last forty years—they have unraveled. And in nearly every case, the delta between the upper class and middle class hasn't just expanded,

FIGURE 3.1

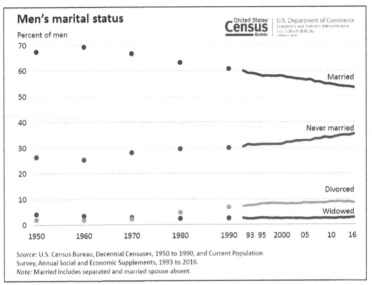

Source: U.S. Census Bureau, Decennial Censuses, 1950 to 1990, and Current Population Survey, Annual Social and Economic Supplements, 1993 to 2016.
Note: Married includes separated and married spouse absent.

it's been blown out. Unmarried men living at their parents' homes, birth rates, divorce rates, marriage rates—in every category over the last forty years, the statistics have worsened for white middle-class and lower-class America and have largely remained unchanged or improved for upper-class America. Today, only 46 percent of American children live with both birth parents, down from 61 percent in 1980 and 73 percent in 1960.[8] Fully 34 percent of children today live with an unmarried parent, up from only 9 percent in 1960 (Figs. 3.2, 3.3).[9]

The Disappearing Able-Bodied American Male

One need not hold to "puritanical" views of marriage and family to recognize the critical role family structure plays in a productive society. Not only is the statistical correlation between strong

FIGURE 3.2

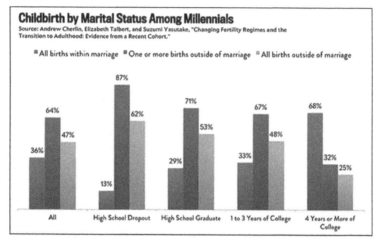

Childbirth by Marital Status Among Millennials
Source: Andrew Cherlin, Elizabeth Talbert, and Suzumi Yasutake, "Changing Fertility Regimes and the Transition to Adulthood: Evidence from a Recent Cohort."

■ All births within marriage ■ One or more births outside of marriage ■ All births outside of marriage

FIGURE 3.3

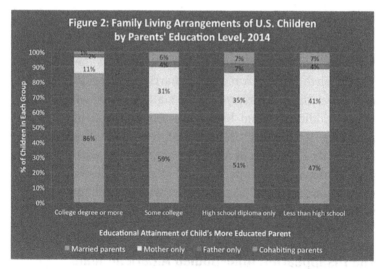

Figure 2: Family Living Arrangements of U.S. Children by Parents' Education Level, 2014

family units and prosperous families undeniable, but the social construct is also intuitive and easy to understand. Marriage creates responsibilities—*civilizing* responsibilities. In addition to being an economic unit of shared resources, the family becomes a vehicle for instilling values, sharing experiences, and learning moral cooperation. Marriage can often be a miracle cure, creating a middle-class family out of two individuals from a lower economic class. The economics (and social forces) behind even two poor people marrying each other means less poverty and more access to the middle class.[10]

There is plenty of reasonable debate to be had about what these various data points do and do not mean. Statistics often force difficult discussions about correlation versus causation, but few sociologists entertain the idea that declining marriages, nuclear families, and children born in wedlock is anything other than a net negative for the economic and emotional well-being of society. I'm not writing a book on the merits of strong marriages or healthy and happy homes for kids, but I would hope all would agree that to aspire for both is a good thing. The more relevant point here is the decline of both amongst those who feel "left out" by the economic advancements of the past quarter century. These declining social conditions (and the decision making that leads to them) are decreasing access to opportunity for middle America.

The best retort to my claim would be to counter that it is the decreasing access to opportunity that is causing the decline in social conditions. It's not true, but it can create a "chicken or egg" stalemate if left unchallenged. By this theory, men are remaining dependent on their parents, often well into their thirties, *because of* the challenging economic conditions they face. Thus, the thinking goes, obsessive video game use and eight-hour-per-day television watching is the *consequence* of what is happening in working-class America, not the cause.

This response should strike most reasonable people as patently absurd, for surely human history has recorded many millennia of men facing extraordinary challenge and economic frustration. Yet never has the response to adversity resulted in an extended, even unending adolescence. In fact, the historical norm has been quite the opposite. When faced with wretched economic conditions and perilous adversity, men's character was enhanced as they embraced hard work and a rugged individualism that would be totally foreign to today's culture. The virtues and industrious sensibilities deep in the American DNA have been progressively numbed since the 1960s, and the result is a declining social fabric worsened by the complexities of modern life. That numbing is most evident in the very places most prone to struggle in the realities of a new, global economy.

These conditions feed upon each other in a vicious cycle that does irreparable harm and intensifies the need to pursue re-moralization—to seek stronger social binds and a renewed sense of family, community, and industriousness. A broken-down family structure obstructs efforts to overcome poverty in every generation, for every civilization, throughout all history. The negative feedback loop is daunting: a collapsed family structure leads to a collapsed work ethic, which leads to a more daunting family environment, which leads to an even more daunting economic reality. There is no self-correcting mechanism in this cycle, other than flight. When a determined "exception to the rule" individual leaves the pain and toxicity of a daunting environment, he or she may leave the dysfunctional situation behind to create a flourishing dynamic and a new reality. But, this also further widens the gap between performance and productivity (virtue and character) in those areas where social conditions have broken down. This has been a very real cycle in American life for over two decades.

This change in the able-bodied American male in less than one generation captures the gravity of what I am describing in the decline of middle America's social fabric. The proponent of strong families and marriages in me finds the aforementioned data points deeply concerning, but the financial economist in me finds the data around increased manipulation of disability claims downright horrifying. Alas, it is impossible to conclude that the two subjects are not significantly more correlated than any of us would want to believe. In 1990, less than 2.5 percent of working-age Americans claimed disability from the Social Security Disability Insurance Trust Fund. Today, the number is over 5.2 percent and climbing (Fig. 3.4).

In the same period of time that medical advancements and medicinal innovations grew exponentially, the percentage of our population unable to work and requiring government financial

FIGURE 3.4

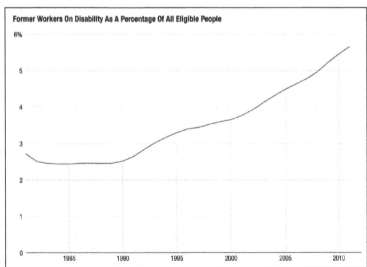

*Social Security Administration, Lam Thuy Vo, NPR.

assistance due to a medical "disability" *more than doubled!* Any objective, rational person must find those two conflicting trends to be irreconcilable aside from the explanation that fraud, an unwillingness to work, and a comfort with exploiting the system have become socially acceptable. The percentage of disability claims around circulatory issues, respiratory issues, parasitic diseases, and other such medically objective problems have declined. Meanwhile, disability claims related to "musculoskeletal" challenges (i.e., back pain) have skyrocketed, as have "nervous system" issues (i.e., anxiety). We now have nearly nine million workers on Social Security disability (fig. 3.5) with cash payments that exceed the cost of food stamps and welfare combined—and what seems to be a legal way to skirt work requirements in the welfare code.

Are many of these claims completely legitimate and outside the scope of the point I'm making? Of course. But no credible source believes that people are not taking advantage of the

FIGURE 3.5

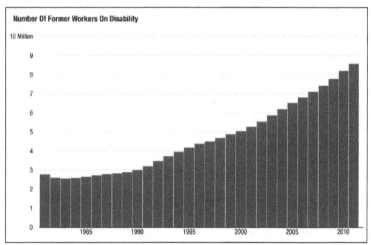

*Social Security Administration, Lam Thuy Vo, NPR

American disability system. It is not only an economic calamity (though it surely is that). The moral climate of Americans only one generation ago would have never tolerated the systemic use of government (or employer) disability programs to avoid work responsibilities.

The Beginning of a Prescription

If Charles Murray's *Coming Apart* in 2012 was the statistical and sociological setup for the political consummation of what is taking place in our society due to this crisis of responsibility, J. D. Vance's *Hillbilly Elegy: A Memoir of a Family and Culture in Crisis* in 2016 was its biography. Vance didn't use a partisan message in this compelling bestseller, but pointedly told the Right to stop telling broken-down communities that the conditions they face are the government's fault:

> I once ran into an old acquaintance at a Middletown bar who told me that he had recently quit his job because he was sick of waking up early. I later saw him complaining on Facebook about the "Obama economy" and how it had affected his life. I don't doubt that the Obama economy has affected many, but this man is assuredly not among them. His status in life is directly attributable to the choices he's made, and his life will improve only through better decisions. But for him to make better choices, he needs to live in an environment that forces him to ask tough questions about himself. There is a cultural movement in the white working class to blame problems on society or the government, and that movement gains adherents by the day.[11]

I couldn't possibly do justice to the correlation between social responsibility and economic vulnerability in one chapter. But those who believe middle America is the victim of an impersonal global economy are ignoring the fact that we've seen a 108 percent increase in working-age Americans living off a government disability check over the last twenty-five years, to list but one inconvenient truth.

It would be reckless and idealistic to conclude that what the Rust Belt, Deep South, or Appalachia needs is merely to buck up and stay married (or get married) in order to see jobs and opportunities quickly flood back into their towns. Various geographic regions of the country have been disproportionately affected by changes in global economic conditions. The advent of cheaper labor in certain foreign countries didn't impact Newport Beach, California, the same way it did factory towns in Ohio.

The policy prescriptions of this book will have much to say about reigniting opportunity in those areas most impacted by shifting economic realities. However, every policy prescription I, or those much smarter than I, could craft will be worth less than the paper on which it is written if the cultural and social context isn't also vastly improved in those areas.

Put differently, you will not write a jobs bill, tax bill, or a trade treaty that means a hill of beans to a community struggling to find able-bodied men willing to work (or able to pass the drug test required for them to get hired). No effort from a civil magistrate will ever succeed in overcoming the malaise created by apathy, irresponsibility, and imploded family norms. We cannot ignore policy prescriptions, yet we must establish a sine qua non—a failure to ignite re-moralization and recapture industriousness, honesty, family, and religion will guarantee the failure of any attempt to improve civic life.

The willingness of the Right to pretend that there isn't a moral rot in middle America fertilizing this crisis of responsibility is counterproductive, to say the least. Conservatives have (accurately, in my view) passionately declared that the West cannot win the war against Islamic jihadist fanaticism if we will not properly identify it as such. I would argue that the same need for self-awareness and an honest diagnosis exists in addressing economic malaise. The crisis of individual responsibility is not going to be fixed by government policy.

By suggesting social deterioration is at the root of the crisis we face, I realize I invite the burden of prescribing solutions to the problem. I am keenly aware that poor factory towns won't see a resurgence of faithful marriages simply because a few sociologists or economists identify the declining family unit as the primary source of economic angst. I am, however, more sympathetic to J. D. Vance's sentiment that solutions begin with initially acknowledging the real problem. We can treat the symptoms, but a cure requires a reprioritization of values and character. The practical ways to get there are few and far between, but important nonetheless.

Charles Murray suggested that part of the problem exacerbating the "coming apart" between upper-class America and the rest is that while the highly educated and professionally successful are *themselves* statistically more likely to be in happy marriages and invest great effort into child-rearing, there is a remarkable failure to "preach what they practice." What's en vogue today is a nonjudgmental attitude about how other people live their lives. That attitude must end. The need of the hour is for thoughtful and caring people to condemn deadbeat-ism, not enable it.

The moral relativism of our age has created a tricky dilemma. Many people are thriving because they're making wise decisions that lead to more fulfilled lives, but they're unwilling to declare wise decision making as a necessary prerequisite for the success of others. Practicing what one preaches is a long-heralded virtue; but preaching what one practices is the mandate for today.

There is no shortage of books on the market prescribing character and virtue as the antidote to what plagues our society. That's a good thing. Principles of self-reliance, responsibility over entitlement, thrift, and the virtues of hard work require a resurgence of popularity. Ben Sasse's landmark *The Vanishing American Adult* suggests that fighting "passivity" and allowing young people to rediscover their "agency" is vital. There are dozens of reasons, from the economic to the physical, that this is true, but none are more potent than the moral and spiritual. A culture that has prized agency over passivity in the past, and seen the positive results in the lives and communities of the educated and elite, has failed to prize those values consistently today across all of society.

We have taken a generation to get to the point we where we now find ourselves societally, and I have no reason to believe we will reverse course in less than another generation. Nevertheless, those who care for the disenfranchised will never pretend that there is one set of rules and norms that work for the privileged few, and a different set of rules and norms for the rest. When we find our voice as a society to sing the praises of family, character, and goodness, we will find the beginning of a prescription for reversing social and economic stagnation.

4

OCCUPY MAIN STREET
The Moral Confusion
of Vindicating the Culprit

Covetousness bursts the sack and spills the grain.

—SIR WALTER SCOTT

It is a positively glorious ride—the ferry across the Hudson River from the World Financial Center Terminal in Manhattan to the Paulus Hook port in Jersey City. Unfortunately, it's only a few minutes long, but it carries a lot of nostalgic value for me.

When I first entered the financial world about twenty years ago, I did a training program in Weehawken, New Jersey, with my then-employer UBS PaineWebber. The ferry ride between Weehawken and Manhattan became a mainstay then. To this day it is impossible for me to be in that vicinity without overpowering memories. When I first entered the business, it was the most exciting, intimidating, nerve-wracking, curious, and thrilling time of my life. Two hundred trips to New York City later, and having opened an office for my company there, nothing has changed. I remain tremendously passionate about the financial markets around which I've built my career.

However, one particular ferry ride toward Jersey City in October 2011 stands out. At that point, we were well over two years removed from the bottom of the market and what many in our business recorded as the "end of the crisis," referring to that March 2009 moment when markets did finally hit bottom and equity prices began to recover. We were three years distant from the Lehman events of September 2008, yet public outcry over the financial crisis had not reached its apex. As I exited to the boardwalk in front of 90 Hudson Street in Jersey City where my meeting was that day, I met that public angst face-to-face.

The boardwalk off the ferry was the entry point from Manhattan to Exchange Place in Jersey City (a sort of secondary Wall Street hub), where financial entities from Goldman Sachs to Merrill Lynch to Morgan Stanley all have prominent offices. Thus it was a logical spot for the now infamous Occupy Wall Street movement to set up shop.

"Give me back my house!" one protester screamed at me, just inches from my face.

"I didn't take your house," I naively responded, thinking he actually wanted a conversation.

"You guys got bailed out! Where is our bailout?"

I suppose he could be forgiven for presuming I worked for a financial firm. I was wearing an expensive suit, carrying an expensive briefcase, and taking the financial center ferry from Wall Street to Exchange Place. His accusations had prima facie support in optics, if not in substance. But I could see it wasn't going to be a worthwhile conversation for me to explain that I worked in wealth management, that my day-to-day work was advising clients on their own capital and decision making. It would also have been pointless to explain that the firms who did extend credit to people who didn't pay their mortgage bills were not exactly in the wrong to retake property that collateralized the bad debt. After engaging him for a minute, it became apparent he probably hadn't even had a house repossessed. Regardless of what I thought about the substance (and hygiene) of the movement, it was merely a symbolic reply to what had gone wrong three years ago.

I politely ended the conversation and continued to my meeting. As expected, Occupy Wall Street faded away shortly thereafter. What has not faded to this day is a public distrust of large financial institutions and a general feeling that "the big guys got off scot-free" and "the little guy got screwed." It isn't a complete picture. In many ways, it isn't totally fair. And in some cases, it is patently false. Nevertheless, it is the consensus view for much of society. If it remains society's default narrative for the crisis of 2008, we all remain vulnerable to a dangerous retelling of the story—a Financial Crisis 2.0, where the same monster simply dons a different mask.

Society's collective response thus far has been a sort of convoluted blame game, divided almost entirely along political lines. Most on the Right have accurately but incompletely focused their attentions on the flaws of government housing policy. A subset has gone after Fannie Mae and Freddie Mac for their excesses. Another subset has focused on the broader social policy objectives so instrumental in driving the housing mania. Still another subset has focused on easy monetary policy that proved to be gasoline thrown on the housing crisis fire. None of them are wrong, per se; they just aren't enough. They are an incomplete assessment of the big picture necessary for a crisis of this magnitude.

Likewise on the Left, targets vary from inadequate regulation to breaking up the big banks, but there is neither a complete assessment of what really went wrong before 2008, nor a proper framework for making sure it never happens again. In this convoluted blame game, we've managed to further polarize society, while doing virtually nothing to solidify a strategy for avoiding another crisis. If we're going to offer constructive, preventative measures, we must cure our polarizing addiction to blame.

In a sense, I advocate the "perfect storm" theory of the crisis—*all* of the elements did play a role in forming the bubble and *all* contributed to the economic catastrophes that resulted from it. However, other analysts of the crisis have not sought to identify *all* the culprits, but rather *the* culprit—the sine qua non, or guilty party, of which it can be said that there would have been no crisis had *this* decision, force, or policy not existed.

Is it possible that every aforementioned culprit served as a sine qua non in this experience? Perhaps. But the particular and consistent theme all shared, the one that was present in each and every element of each and every guilty party, was an underlying spirit of *envy*. The green-eyed monster seized the opportunity created by an absence of character, the presence of the intemperate cravings, and utter disdain for the virtues of patience and thrift. No part of our culture was immune. Not Wall Street. Not K Street. And, especially, not Main Street.

Monsters on Main Street

Monsters sometimes wear masks. As all parents know, the time for masks is Halloween, and it was on such a night in 2005 that my wife, Joleen, and I attended a party prior to having children of our own. In this gated community in Orange County, California, parties and elegant houses are the norm, but this party was truly over the top.

We were attending as friends of friends, so we didn't even know the new owners' names. They had clearly spared no expense. As we walked into the home through a grand foyer with soaring ceilings, we were wowed by custom inlay marble floors. From the foyer, we could see most of the 8,000-square-foot home. Not a square inch of custom wrought-iron lighting lacked elaborate Halloween décor. The twelve-person surround-sound home theater played scary Halloween videos as guests balanced cocktails, trying not to spill on the French oak floors. The 1,100-bottle wine cellar grabbed a lot of attention, as did the light show in the backyard displaying images of ghosts and goblins.

I vacillated between staring at the Halloween party décor and the stunning wood-carved crown molding. I heard the host tell numerous guests that the hardwood was all imported and they wouldn't see any other flooring throughout the home other than custom Italian marble. The home's style was old-world Tuscan— far from my taste, frankly. The host informed each person how "custom" the style was, despite the fact that nearly every home in the community was being built the same way.

When the deluxe game room with wet bar became a "guy's hangout," I resigned there after touring the entire home. It was a nice home, but if you've seen one Venetian plaster wall, you've seen them all. As I sat down, I tuned into a conversation between two gentlemen next to me.

"Did you hear he pulled $100k from his HELOC for this party," said one man I'd never seen before to the friend sitting next to him.

"Yes," his friend replied, "he said they almost pulled more but didn't want to get *too* crazy."

"My wife and I just paid $1.6 [million] for our new pad this summer," the first man replied. "Agent says we can nab $1.9 now. I can tell you for sure my wife will have us home shopping tomorrow after this party."

He sounded neither totally excited, nor totally dejected as he continued, "When we bought our first home for $700k four years ago, I was so stretched—you have no idea! Now it's time to break $2 million, and I haven't put a single dollar into any of the last three homes besides what we've flipped. This market is *hot*, but it just kills me that I am on house number four and here this guy comes in and shows us all up with this beast! I liked our house when I bought it, but now it's *embarrassing.*"

I don't know if this gentleman and his wife went shopping for homes the next day or not. If they did, they would probably have been able to buy a $2 million plus home with nothing down at the time. They would have received multiple offers to buy their current "embarrassment" within just a few days. Such was the easy housing market in the years before 2008.

The flips continued for another year, with artificial equity being rolled into new homes to make mortgage notes feel manageable. Low interest rates helped monthly payments feel serviceable. In a more normal world, I suspect the income of this gentleman would have been more appropriate for a $700k to $1.25 million home (and even that assumes a low-interest-rate environment). But these were not normal times, and circumstances allowed the home sticker price for folks like this gentleman to exceed $2 million.

This scenario was common in Orange County and all around the country. Although the dollar figures varied market to market, American families had become engrossed in a frenetic game of "keeping up with the Joneses," a game that had gotten completely out of hand as they fed the insatiable, green-eyed monster.

As my neighbors—and yours—rushed to flip houses from Irvine to Iowa, another conversation occurred on Forty-Eighth Street and Seventh Avenue in midtown Manhattan. There in 2005 and 2006, Dick Fuld, CEO of Lehman Brothers, sat atop the forty-first floor of a spectacular office metropolis. *Fortune* magazine had just run a puff piece on him that is now (with the gift of hindsight) painful to read. Fuld was an ambitious man, a competitive man, who had certainly done some impressive things after taking over as CEO after 1994. No one doubted Fuld's tenacity, though we now know more of his aloofness and even arrogance. But other forces were at work in that high-rise office, forces not all that different from the conversation I overheard at my neighbor's elaborate Halloween party.

"These guys won't let up," Fuld said, referring to a series of high-profile real estate purchases that his former rivals had recently made (Stephen Schwarzman and Pete Peterson of private equity behemoth Blackstone). "I don't care what it takes—I want it," continued Fuld, referring to the Coeur Défense office complex in central Paris that Lehman closed on a short time later for the not-so-bargain-basement price of $2.9 billion.[12]

When the deal closed in 2007, it represented the highest price paid for office space ever in the history of humanity. Did this particular $2.9 billion office acquisition sink Lehman Brothers? Of course not. And that particular gated-community conversation didn't sink the U.S. housing market, either. But the shared monstrous mentality behind both conversations set the scene for the disastrous financial collapse that followed.

There is not one iota of difference between the conversation at the Halloween party in Irvine and the one on the forty-first floor in Manhattan. The dollar amounts and economic implications may vary on the surface, but the monster at the core is the same—*envy*. While one is of a more institutional variety (corporate envy in the halls of Lehman) and one is of a more retail variety (neighborhood envy of "keeping up with the Joneses"), both capture the root cause of the 2008 financial crisis in a word we don't hear much anymore: *covetousness*.

The truth is this: while Wall Street was riddled with both covetous greed and arrogant incompetence, no financial crisis of any kind could have taken place without the envious and covetous irresponsibility of the people living on good old Main Street, USA. The biblical edict of "thou shalt not covet thy neighbor's house" may be ancient, but it proved most prescient in 2008.

The aspiration for a better house is not to be condemned, but mere upward mobility was not the story behind the real estate bubble of 2000 to 2007. It was a reckless mobility driven by an epidemic of instant gratification. Artificially inflated real estate prices gave way to even more artificially inflated prices, and a society of desperate perpetrators used various financial machinations to get more right now "because my friend has it."

When mobility and aspiration meet patience, diligence, hard work, thrift, and investment, the result is often a better house, new floors, a nice Halloween party, and all such luxuries of an abundant life. But when aspiration is driven simply to impress others, and to do so by substituting the aforementioned virtues for haste, sloppiness, and financial irresponsibility, the result is disastrous.

The Subprime Housing Myth

Before we proceed, it is important to bury a myth that has implicitly (and often explicitly) been included in nearly every narrative of the financial crisis, despite it being mathematically absurd. It is the myth that "subprime" housing loans caused the crisis.

For this discussion, I am defining "subprime" as those cases where people of very low income and credit quality bought highly overpriced houses with very risky loans and lost those houses when the payments became too much to bear. If one defines "subprime" more broadly as any form of nontraditional mortgage, the theory becomes more reasonable, but the buyers and borrowers at the heart of the 14 million crisis of home foreclosures were not merely those extreme cases of a $35,000/year gardener buying a $500,000 home. At the heart of the financial crisis were millions of people who could afford their home payment, but realized that the sticker price they paid was far more than the present resale value of the home, and thus made the morally questionable decision to walk away.

My intent is not to parse the wisdom or lack thereof in each individual circumstance, but rather to allow the data to reveal the inescapable conclusion. The bubble-like behavior—while doused with kerosene by a reckless monetary policy, accelerated by a dangerous government housing agenda, enabled by a failed regulatory framework, and facilitated by a short-sighted and incompetent financial system—was still fundamentally at its root a byproduct of human irresponsibility in a culture of insufficient thrift and virtue.

For our purposes, I'll divide "Main Street" into several categories. Just as "Wall Street" is too broad of a term to use to refer to all mortgage lenders, rating agencies, investment bankers, traders, risk managers, hedge fund managers, CEOs, and commercial bankers (each of whom played a role in the crisis, but none of whom owned the entire supply chain of the irresponsible financial action that took place), so "Main Street" requires greater specificity.

The media and broader societal narrative has defined "Main Street" as "the victim" and "Wall Street" as "the perpetrator," thus allowing a prebaked conclusion to the question at hand. But since very few sensible people believe Goldman Sachs forced a homebuyer or mortgage borrower to take out a loan, and even fewer people believe they (or any other Wall Street firm) forced homebuyers *not to fulfill their obligations on the loan*, it behooves us to dig deeper into what roles each actor played.

The Main Street Players

We can think of the Main Street players as four unique actors:

1. **The Swindled.** These actors were the very poor and naïve who truly did not understand any part of what they were doing when they signed loan documents obligating them to payments they could not afford. In short, they were duped by predatory lenders.

53

2. **The Reckless.** These people irresponsibly encumbered themselves through mortgages or cash-out borrowing they could not afford. But they understood the risk associated and proceeded anyway, out of either the belief that continuously rising home prices would fix everything or out of callous disregard for consequences.

3. **The Gamblers.** This group was financially capable and reasonably educated. They rolled the dice and speculated all the way. When they lost the bet, they recognized the economic convenience of a strategic default. They chose to walk away from their obligations with the presumption that there would be no negative consequences to their income or balance sheet. And they were right.

4. **The Diligent.** The final players were those who missed no payments in the financial crisis and, therefore, added no stress to the financial system. They faithfully made the payments they had promised to make.

The Diligent bear no responsibility for the financial crisis for the obvious reason that they fulfilled (and continue to fulfill) their financial responsibilities. In an indirect way, however, they may deserve some criticism for being inadequately agitated at the Reckless and the Gamblers. The Diligent seem to lack an appreciation for just how unfair the actions of the other players really were. Instead, many have joined the chorus criticizing easy institutional targets of earlier chapters. But my desire for righteous indignation doesn't address the culpability of the other Main Street players, so I focus on the remaining three.

Predatory Lending: The Swindled

Research indicates that some people were swindled. There were incidents of fraud and predatory deceit, but those cases were outliers. To be sure, the media has had a field day with these outliers, but the reality is that total mortgage losses suffered during the financial crisis were roughly $1 trillion. Yet losses from bank-perpetrated fraud of indigent or mentally unaware consumers are estimated to not be even a drop in that bucket.

To clarify, being an unqualified borrower targeted for loans does not include one in the Swindled. Unscrupulous dealers (the mortgage brokers) often *were* on one side of these transactions with buyers (the borrowers). We've already established that many involved in the supply chain didn't care about what was best for the borrower, what was best for the lender, and certainly not what was best for the overall financial system. However, when I talk about the Swindled, I refer to instances where lenders actually lied to customers about the interest rate or cost of the mortgage, where documents were manipulated, and where papers were being force-fed to a borrower who could not be expected to legally or morally comprehend what was happening.

There is little data available as to how often these most severe cases took place, but what we can know is that: (1) where these incidents did take place, they represent a perverse violation of business ethics and human decency; and (2) they were not anything close to being a systemic factor in the overall financial crisis. It is impossible to know what degree of financial sophistication these borrowers had, but the notion that over ten million mortgage borrowers representing well over $700 billion of borrowing were people without even a basic understanding of monthly payments or total debt liability simply defies imagination.

The Swindled group does not include people who showed general irresponsibility (poor spending disciplines, broad financial naiveté, confused monetary priorities, etc.). Those people rightly deserve to be labeled as the Reckless. The Swindled refers to those cases where any reasonable person would see the borrower as a victim—where there was paper switching, direct lying, exploitation of language deficiencies, mental incapacity, and so forth. Let's acknowledge that rare and despicable incidents such as these took place, but at nowhere near the level required to fuel a financial crisis.

Predatory Borrowing: The Reckless and The Gamblers

The sad reality is that predatory *borrowing* was a far more systemic problem than predatory *lending*. The fact is that 70 percent of defaulted loans had *blatant* misrepresentations on their mortgage applications.[13] The FBI estimates that mortgage fraud (by borrowers) increased *1,000 percent* from 2001 to 2007. In other words, borrowers frequently made false claims to get loans, yet why did that reality not become part of the postcrisis narrative? Why is "predatory lending" a commonly used term, whereas "predatory borrowing" is the odd contraption of a free market economist? (Tyler Cowen of George Mason University used the term early on in the financial crisis.) The reason is simple: *the facts do not agree with the created narrative.*

If we combined all predatory loans—cases where the lender perpetrated fraud against the borrower by deceiving him or her about the loan—and all cases of predatory borrowing—cases where the borrower perpetrated fraud against the lender—we still have only 25 percent of the total defaults in the financial crisis according to the *Journal of Financial Economics.*[14] That means 75 percent of all defaults came from people who did legitimately qualify for a loan yet defaulted anyway—the Reckless and the Gamblers.

I suspect most readers know someone in one of these categories. I'm using a broad brush here because macroeconomics deals with macro circumstances, with broad economic trends, and with numbers that apply across certain classes and segments. No doubt I'll step on some micro toes when discussing these macro events. Certain specific situations may very well have had exigent circumstances that paint a more sympathetic picture than my broad categories allow. I beg your pardon where those situations exist and ask for the benefit of the doubt as we examine some harsh realities.

The Gamblers are most likely to engender irritation and least likely to gain your sympathy. Some were extremely bad actors, confident they could speculate en masse, keeping 100 percent of any upside and passing along 100 percent of any downside to their lending institutions and, eventually, to the taxpayers. In other cases that I would still include with the Gamblers, the intent may not have been as sinister, the volume of transactions may have been lower, or financial objectives may not have been based on rank speculation—and yet the end result was the same.

An intelligent and financially capable borrower simply walked away from debt they *could* afford. This morally questionable activity was *not* rare. It was commonplace. And this activity did *not* have a *minor* financial impact. The Gamblers on Main Street were *major* actors in the financial crisis drama.

The national credit bureau Experian worked with the consulting outfit Oliver Wyman in late 2009 to conduct an analysis on these strategic defaults.[15] The results were damning for the Gamblers. Using a sample of twenty-four million credit files, they found that borrowers with *high* credit scores were 50 percent *more likely* to strategically default, thus debunking the myth that it was less creditworthy and capable people struggling through the financial crisis. They also discovered these sorts of events— the abandonment of a mortgage obligation to pay *when people were perfectly able to pay*—represented fully 20 to 30 percent of the delinquencies that took place in 2007 and 2008 (a jaw-dropping one million incidents in these two years alone, with these incidents accelerating into 2009). After evaluating the other patterns and activities in the credit reports, the analysis indicated that the perpetrators were "clearly sophisticated."

Another damning study from economists at the University of Chicago and Northwestern University[16] found that those who personally knew someone else who had strategically defaulted made *them* 82 percent more likely to do so, demonstrating the lack of social stigma effect: *if they did it, I can do it too*. It pegged the percentage of strategic defaults as 26 percent of the national default levels. Wealthy communities were not remotely immune from the Gamblers' misdeeds—in fact, they were the sweet spot for such activity. California saw strategic defaults multiply *by a factor of 68 and Florida by a factor of 46!* Meanwhile other states with lower median incomes saw their rates multiply only by a factor of 9.[17] The delinquency rate for mortgages *above* $1 million reached 23 percent in the aftermath of the crisis, but it stayed at 10 percent for mortgages *below* $1 million. Perhaps wealthier people were more ruthless and reckless, but they also had more resources. Clearly it was not the poor and needy who led the rush off the cliff of strategic defaults.

When Monsters Wear Masks

The proof for the Gamblers' existence on Main Street and their role in first creating and then exacerbating the financial crisis can be found in two empirical facts:

1. 41 percent of all mortgage defaults took place in California and Florida, states that mandated nonrecourse financing (meaning, the *borrowers could not be held personally liable* for a failure to perform on their mortgage loans). In fact, the vast majority of all mortgage defaults came in nonrecourse lending states. Are we to believe that the exact conditions blamed for the financial crisis

somehow magically plagued these few states, with no correlation to the fact that these states allowed borrowers to walk away scot-free?

2. To help borrowers who claimed challenges in making their monthly payment, loan modifications became a huge craze in the aftermath of the crisis (i.e., loan terms were restructured to make the monthly payment more favorable to the borrower, whether through a changed interest rate, an extension of term, or a forbearance on principal payment). However, something stunning happened:

  a. 36 percent of those who received a modification to their loan defaulted *again* in just three months[18]

  b. 58 percent defaulted *again* within eight months[19]

  c. 67 percent defaulted *again* within eighteen months[20]

Why would a borrower who had gone through the trouble of getting a loan reworked to provide relief and an easier payment default anyway? Because at the end of the day, the value of the asset was worth less than the debt they were servicing on that asset. And so approximately one million borrowers walked away, despite having received favorable options to alleviate the anxiety around their monthly payment. An entirely new term for what we used to call failure to perform was created—the aforementioned "strategic default." (Millions more "strategically defaulted," but I am highlighting here those who received favorable relief on their loans in some capacity, and yet defaulted shortly thereafter anyway.)

The conclusion is impossible to ignore: the vast majority of strategic defaults came from people who had the resources to pay (and, in fact, had been given grace and financial assistance) yet still chose to walk away because they realized there would be virtually no financial repercussions to them personally. They saw an opportunity to get out from an investment that was upside down—and they took it.

The distinction between the Reckless and the Gamblers may evoke different moral responses. Whereas the Gamblers clearly had the financial capability to pay, the Reckless could no longer cover the debt obligations. And yet they had taken on the obligations with an understanding of the risks involved. So much of the confusion about the Reckless can be blamed on the vocabulary adopted to describe the financial crisis.

The mental imagery of a subprime borrower is one who has no job, no income, no assets, and no credit, yet received a mortgage anyway. The reality is that nearly all data describing the impact of subprime borrowing in the housing bubble includes data of what we might call "near-prime" borrowing, or "Alt-A" lending. While subprime borrowing proved to be harmful in the financial crisis, it was Alt-A lending[21] that proved catastrophic.

Alt-A was the mortgage category that included nontraditional lending, but not necessarily to subprime, severely credit-impaired borrowers. The Federal Reserve's own data on the subject shows roughly a 70 percent growth in subprime issuance from 2003 to 2005 (as the hot real estate market was becoming the bubble of all bubbles). But the same data also shows a stunning *360 percent growth in that same time period for Alt-A loans.*

Much has been said about the roughly 20 percent default rate in subprime borrowing by the summer of 2008. Indeed, a 20 percent default rate is higher than the 10 percent default rate Alt-A loans were experiencing by that same summer. However, subprime delinquencies had been in the 5 to 6 percent range just a few years earlier when the housing market was doing well. So, the subprime default increased from 5 to 20 percent, i.e., *by a factor of 4*. However, before the bubble began to pop, Alt-A loans had a virtually 0 percent default rate (0.6 percent to be precise). By the summer of 2008, as the housing market melted down and the crisis began, the 10 percent default rate for Alt-As meant they had multiplied *by a factor of 16!* And from a pure dollars and cents standpoint, the Alt-A issuance throughout the key bubble-formative years of 2002–2006 was exponentially higher than classic subprime issuance. By the end of the bubble, *Alt-A lending represented fully half (50 percent) of new loans issued in the mortgage market* (over $1.4 trillion in 2006 alone), while subprime issuance had peaked at 16 percent of new loans issued.[22]

Significant data supports the fact that this middle ground of Alt-A lending created the most financial distress in the crisis. Yet why have those selling the narrative about the financial crisis gone to such great lengths to intentionally define it as primarily a *subprime* failure? Answer that question and you will understand why I believe this subject gets to the heart of the matter.

The term "subprime" effectively and even dramatically conjures up an image of a victim. They are *sub*-something. Those labeled as *sub*-anything have inferior capabilities. They are disadvantaged from the start. Only a greedy and heartless entity would go after something as helpless as the *sub*prime, right? But by combining all data of "non-prime" (Alt-A and subprime) into one broad category of subprime, these storytellers have effectively poisoned the well in this discourse. If the narrative aligned with reality—a huge amount of totally intelligent and capable borrowers with adequate credit and debt service capabilities took out reckless, irresponsible, and nontraditional loans—*there would be no room for a victimization movement.*

This sleight of hand was not accidental. A massive amount of contaminated loans were at the heart of the capital losses that created the financial crisis. Those contaminated loans were taken out primarily by irresponsible borrowers who *did* have adequate credit and income to service them. It was the loan-to-value ratio—the fact that there was very little protective equity in these types of loans—that gave borrowers of adequate credit and income the economic green light to walk away when conditions changed.

When the source of their default was irresponsible borrowing and spending, a moral indictment is in order. What we do know is that consumer spending increased a stunning 6.9 percent in 2005 over 2004. We know that home equity extraction as a percentage of consumer spending *tripled* in the five years leading up to 2005.[23] Total household debt exploded to 127 percent of household income by 2007. It was the Alt-A mortgage category that enabled this expanded borrowing—and borrow they did.

Fueled by access to more liquidity than they had ever seen, often with tax-deductible interest and always with lower interest rates than other options, reckless borrowers exploded in number in the years 2000–2007. The results were nothing less than utterly catastrophic. Wall Street, Fannie, Freddie, and government policy certainly deserve some blame for giving *access* to this credit, but for *recklessly using* this credit the real blame belongs to the envious among us, right here on Main Street.

Ten Percent Had No Conscience

The consensus view of the financial crisis is that the blame lies with those who made and sold the lending products. Such a view seeks to vindicate those who bought and used the product—an incomplete, inaccurate, and, indeed, morally flawed view of adult responsibility.

A perfect storm of government mandates, irresponsible policy fed down to government agencies, and the incompetent calculations of those in the credit and capital markets created the conditions necessary for this crisis. Indeed, Main Street could not have fed at the trough of easy borrowing, excessive spending, and living beyond one's means without those accomplice actors. However, there has been a trend in our culture for decades to pardon the actual actor and participant in wrongdoing. The housing crisis is but one, albeit painful, example of this trend.

Recent years have seen a societal blame shifting from those drinking excessive amounts of soda to the soft drink companies, not the beverage consumer. We see fast food franchises demonized, and not those ordering and eating the food. Certainly there is a parallel with the tobacco companies, as well. My intent is not to fully vindicate all the corporate activity we observe. Corporate America shares a responsibility to be good corporate citizens, and in a free and virtuous society, our great companies should exercise that responsibility with appropriate focus on consumer options, consumer education, and integrity. However, the idea that all bad acting which takes place in society is the responsibility of those providing the raw material and not of those doing the acting is an idea that will undermine the entire strength and will of our culture over time. Such a view of moral agency overturns traditional values and makes victims of perpetrators.

Yet, this misguided view has governed the consensus narrative of the financial crisis and the Great Recession that followed. We're asked to believe that the *availability* of bad loans is the problem, and the institutions making these bad loans *available* are the problem—but not the people *taking* them, and not the people *failing to pay* on them. A society with more moral intuition would never allow the prima facie response to be disgusted with those who lent the money instead of with those who refused to pay it back. And when the actor not making good on the debts so often had adequate, or even abundant, financial resources, this lack of moral clarity becomes even more appalling.

We are right to look upon the actions of Dick Fuld and his cohorts at Lehman Brothers negatively for excessively irresponsible acquisitions, purchases, and leveraging in the years that led up to the financial crisis. The economic ramifications were disastrous, and the moral pathology at play was beyond the pale. And yet, why should our response to an essentially identical moral pathology from Main Street be any different? Is what's sauce for the goose also sauce for the gander, even if the gander doesn't wear Armani suits or work on Park Avenue? Our communities in the culture and ethos of American life were filled with those living above their means, at varying degrees of self-awareness, as thrift very often became obsolete. There was a crisis of culture in the events that created the crisis, a covetous envy in the society-wide game of "keeping up with the Joneses." And there was a crisis of culture that exacerbated the crisis, walking away from obligations without concern for personal integrity or collective economic impact.

Wall Street's use of the synthetic CDO—an investment device used to bet that mortgage bonds would perform and that Americans would keep paying their house payments—proved to be a weapon of mass destruction for our financial system. But no exotic CDO bet caused any Americans to quit paying their bills. Wall Street's error was not in causing Americans on Main Street to stop paying their bills, but in making the wrong bet as to whether or not they would.

In October of 2009, I sat in the thirty-fifth floor conference room in the Fifth Avenue offices of one of the premier credit hedge funds in the industry. As I talked to the portfolio manager about the crazy twelve months we had just experienced, he said one of the most chilling things I have ever heard. "We had a financial crisis, David," he said to me, "because 10 percent of the society had no conscience. The financial crisis only ended because it proved to be 10 percent and not 20 percent."

The implication was clear. Ten percent of the population walking away from responsibility was enough to cause the crisis. We managed to barely emerge from the other side at 10 percent. Had the number been 20 percent, we would not have been so lucky. Yet have the moral scruples of society improved since the financial crisis or worsened? Wall Street has been forced to deleverage and now incurs a web of regulatory oversight that borders on the obnoxious. But what about the monster on Main Street, that green-eyed spirit of envy that drove so many of the people in neighborhoods with cul-de-sacs and picket fences to risk total economic collapse for *just a little bit more*? Has Main Street's moral compass been deleveraged?

How we respond to *that* question as a society will determine whether 2008 was a painful memory in our economic history, or a foreshadowing of darker times to come.

5

THE ROBOTS ARE COMING

What Free Trade and Automation Mean for the American Worker

It is the maxim of every prudent master of a family, never to attempt to make at home what it will cost him more to make than to buy. The tailor does not attempt to make his own shoes, but buys them of the shoemaker. The shoemaker does not attempt to make his own clothes, but employs a tailor. The farmer attempts to make neither the one nor the other, but employs those different artificers. All of them find it for their interest to employ their whole industry in a way in which they have some advantage over their neighbors, and to purchase with a part of its produce, or what is the same thing, with the price of a part of it, whatever else they have occasion for. What is prudence in the conduct of every private family can scarce be folly in that of a great kingdom.

—ADAM SMITH

If you think of opportunity in terms of the Gold Rush, then you'd be pretty depressed right now because the last nugget of gold would be gone. But the good thing is, with innovation, there isn't a last nugget. Every new thing creates two new questions and two new opportunities.

—JEFF BEZOS

If there is one area that has provided prima facie emotional support to the plight of those who feel left out of the new global economy, it has been the impact of free trade and global economic exchange. The narrative is a powerful one of a blue-collar worker losing a job—and worse, value in the marketplace—as cheap foreign labor replaces his or her skill set. It evokes great emotion and sympathy—and so it should. We shouldn't ignore the impact of trade policy and market interventions on real people in real communities who are simply seeking to be part of a virtuous humanity. Policymakers have a fiduciary responsibility to seek an optimal framework for civic life.

It diminishes the credibility of free trade advocates (like myself) to deny that in particular cases and specific circumstances, the advent of a globalized economy has created challenges or pain. Free traders such as me assert that, in a macro sense, the free exchange of products, services, and even labor has dramatically benefitted the economy. (In this sense I do mean the domestic U.S. economy, though I would also argue the same for the global economy). Nevertheless, my vehement argument for the macro benefits of global exchange does not negate those individual circumstances where an individual, a family, a neighborhood, or a community experience great angst because of those changes.

Our task is threefold: (1) understand what has actually transpired across the global economy over the last two decades or so, (2) evaluate the benefits and challenges these developments have created, and (3) suggest a framework by which a responsible society can respond to a rapidly changing world.

The above caution applies both ways. Just as ignoring the distinction between beneficial macro effects and individual micro effects can hinder thoughtful, empathetic analysis, so do attempts to personalize and villainize what are clearly impersonal, economic forces. To say "XYZ low-cost manufacturer in China caused my town's factory to shut down" is a fair statement.

But "globalizing economies are ruining our town's economy" is not. "The Chinese are stealing our jobs" is particularly not helpful—and possibly xenophobic. As any first-year economics student knows, rational capital flocks to its best use.

Moreover, the issue of trade in the global economy is a complex, nuanced topic brought about by a reality that is itself amoral. How economic actors respond to changes may, or may not, have moral implications, but the problem we're trying to solve is not the fact that increased global trade and lower production costs cause disruption in certain sectors. Rather, our agenda is to examine the impact of global free trade with an eye toward a policy prescription. Instead of assigning blame, we need to understand the full spectrum of economic complexity created by these modern developments: free trade, automation, artificial intelligence, and a digitalized economy relying more on information than products and labor.

Doing More with Less

Those who believe easy access to a global labor force caused U.S. companies to import products for less than domestic manufacturing costs must face an inconvenient truth. American manufacturing jobs began declining in both relative and absolute terms decades before NAFTA ever became law. The significant, yet politically uninteresting, fact of the matter is that a dramatic increase in U.S. manufacturing productivity has enabled the sector to *do more with less*. The United States remains the second largest manufacturer in the world, responsible for 17.2 percent of total global output. It is the third largest exporter in the world.[24] America's manufacturing contribution has simply not been the issue, either to her own or the global economy. The issue has been the labor force required to maintain that same level of manufacturing output.

FIGURE 5.1

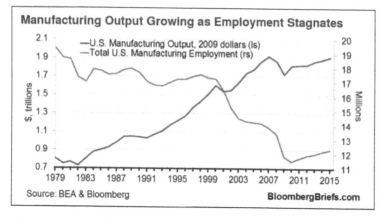

The numbers displayed in figure 5.1 show a thirty-five-year period in which manufacturing output in the U.S. didn't just climb—it grew exponentially, even as employment in the manufacturing sector declined in inverse proportion. NAFTA and other high-profile trade agreements didn't enter the story told by this data until halfway through this timeframe.

Technology, economies of scale, innovation, improved divisions of labor (i.e., specialization)—the American economy has seen a productivity boom, and productivity is the engine of economic growth. The reality is this: if we applied productivity levels in the year 2000 to actual production output in 2010, we would have required nearly twenty-one million workers. But our 2010 production required barely twelve million workers. Our manufacturing output did not decline, but we produced more with dramatically less.[25]

If we choose to view that situation as a problem, we open an incredibly un-American can of worms. We are not, and never have been, a society that celebrates inefficiency. It's perfectly human to bemoan the loss of jobs and the economic anxiety created by improvements in manufacturing productivity, but to bemoan increased productivity and efficiency itself is simply not in the American DNA. Even if the facts don't align with a political narrative, they remain stubborn things. American manufacturing did *not* decline; the number of bodies required did. We can and should celebrate the benefits of greater efficiency, primarily incredible cost savings for consumers. At the same time we recognize the net result on the economy as positive, we should also evaluate the best path forward for the disaffected.

However, let's set aside for now the standard, and perfectly valid, arguments for how consumers have benefitted in this more globalized and technologized economy. It's an argument I clearly accept and, in fact, believe to be often understated. The food and clothing sectors, for example, have benefitted consumers by leveraging increased efficiencies and decreased production costs. A seminal 2015 study by the National Bureau of Economic Research (NBER) found poor and middle-class groups enjoyed 90 percent of the benefits of free trade.[26] The low-cost competition made famous by the likes of Walmart has created incredible convenience and access to low-cost goods for the very economic classes we're talking about better protecting. All of this should be celebrated.

But those on either side of this issue need not deny that certain economic actors derive certain benefits *and yet* certain economic actors also disproportionately suffer. Not only is it an undeniable fact, but candidly acknowledging it to be true does not threaten either side's position!

The market is made with such tensions. The ebb and flow of economics calls for tensions between consumers and producers, importers and exporters, wholesalers and retailers, etc. Lower production costs and greater production efficiencies have given consumers huge gains—yet some of those same consumers have lost their jobs. Falling prices at Walmart is a poor consolation prize for the one displaced by the technological and global developments that made cheaper goods possible. The question, of course, is what to do about it.

Protectionism Pabulum

It is immoral, and dangerously bad economics, to claim that the net economic gain to the whole of society should be less important than the particular economic impact on one specific group of people. Readers familiar with the "broken window fallacy" (made famous by Frédéric Bastiat and popularized by Henry Hazlitt) can imagine where this leads—economic policy based on the *perceived* needs of the few, while ignoring the *actual* needs of the many.

Protectionism usually seeks to protect a small group on the receiving end of an economic disruption. But sustainable economic growth depends on assessing not only short-term impacts, but long-term impacts, as well. Our economic health as a whole cannot be sacrificed for a perceived benefit to a smaller group. Such an approach is morally self-refuting and counterintuitive to our free enterprise system. To make things worse, disdain for global supply chain realities, more efficient production practices, and the leveraging of technological advantages is hurting the very people many well-meaning folks intend to help.

For example, the economic impact of tariffs meant to punish offshore activity is mostly felt by U.S. workers hoping to keep their jobs. Higher production costs, either from the tariff itself or a less efficient production process, results in fewer employees and lower wages. By stifling innovation and productivity and promoting the poor use of the global supply chain, we keep others from working who might otherwise be domestically employed in marketing, sales, design, fulfillment, creative services, packaging, etc. Indeed, when multinational companies hire more foreign employees, they also *increase* domestic hiring.

(Foreign affiliates at U.S. companies rose from 9 million in 2004 to 13.8 million in 2014; meanwhile, the domestic hiring at those exact same companies increased by nearly the same numbers.[27])

The truth is we lack any effective policy lever to force free economic actors to pursue their company's aims in an inefficient way. Protectionist tariffs invite retaliation while creating costs that get passed on to consumers or low-wage laborers. Plus, they don't address the fundamental truth exposed by this paradigm shift: *we need a more adaptable labor force.*

Adapt or Die

Along with the nationalists and protectionists, I empathize with those who feel displaced in the economy. But I do not endorse a policy prescription that claims to help the displaced by enabling them to become even more displaced. The need of the hour is not to ignore the economic advantages and disadvantages created by the free market, but to train, prepare, and equip the disadvantaged with the tools and resources they need to defeat displacement.

The idea of punishing companies for building products more efficiently overseas has even less merit when we consider the more systemic problem of our laborers not developing new job skills, learning new technologies, or adapting to changing market conditions. The responsible thing to do is not to deny changes in the labor market have taken place, or use manipulative tools of the state to alter conditions in the global economy. Rather, the responsible thing to do is to *improve labor dynamism*—the ability of our labor force to adapt and grow in response to free market changes. Improving labor dynamism is a sustainable solution that respects the dignity of the individual while not risking significant interventions in the marketplace, interventions that usually do more harm than good.

Plenty of good apologetics exist for the merits of free trade.[28] In the previous pages, I've attempted only a cursory look at the cause and effect dynamics of free trade in our economy. However, in a book proposing personal responsibility as a significant antidote to the challenges of globalization, the defense of free trade is anecdotal economic education. At a deeper level, we must face the facts that our society faces real challenges, and playing the victimization card puts us at a serious disadvantage. Our crisis of responsibility tempts us to address the microcosms of free trade challenges with protectionist policies. Our crisis of responsibility enables politicians of both parties to promote a fantasy—the idea that political forces can somehow slow or alter technological paradigm shifts moving at the speed of light.

Many people who have seen their life's career skills become obsolete via the disruption of market forces need a significant investment in retraining. These individuals are not victims of a malignant foe intent on harming random strangers; they are bystanders to the inevitable process of change, progress, and dynamism. That doesn't make the impact on them and their families any less real, or any less daunting, but what kind of loving response enables a lie? There are jobs that have been lost in our society that are not coming back—and a substantial part of the disgruntled class knows it, yet continues in the avoidance behavior of victimization. This simply must stop.

Many business leaders and policymakers have introduced mature policy solutions to address these realities, only to see continued grandstanding prevent any real progress. Many disgruntled workers have bemoaned the jobs lost to outsourcing, offshoring, or some other easily demonized force of economic nature, and yet non-farm job openings are at their highest point in recorded history.[29] There simply aren't enough qualified applicants (fig. 5.2). The fields most afflicted? Construction, transportation, and—yes—*manufacturing*. Have the educational requirements and specific vocational criteria changed? Of course. But the minimal level of labor dynamism required to meet that challenge ought not be beneath us as Americans.

In chapter 11, we'll examine practical ways to make labor dynamism more achievable. Public policy can, in certain areas, assist training efforts to prepare workers who are ill-equipped to thrive in the digital or more globalized economy in which we now live. The Cato Institute's Scott Lincicome has done yeoman's work demonstrating several key areas where public policy can improve our efforts in this arena:[30]

- ▶ Allow business training to be tax deductible, even when it is not in one's current field.
- ▶ Significantly reduce regulation in employment, especially termination practices that remove the incentive for healthy labor market flows.
- ▶ Revise the tax code's preference for employer-sponsored health insurance and discriminatory treatment of the individual insurance market.
- ▶ Change a bureaucratic approach to job retraining that has failed miserably.
- ▶ Address the disability programs described in chapter 3, which are facilitating the avoidance of retraining and dynamic preparation for labor productivity.

Our commitment to sympathy should be real and authentic for those disaffected by the challenges of automation, globalization, and changing labor and trade dynamics. It should also motivate us to feed productive ideas—not symbolic or counterproductive ones. Few things in the history of civilization have created more mutually beneficial economic opportunity than free trade. Responding to the challenges that have become painfully transparent in the present political environment need not

FIGURE 5.2

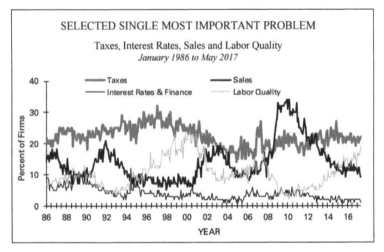

SELECTED SINGLE MOST IMPORTANT PROBLEM

Taxes, Interest Rates, Sales and Labor Quality
January 1986 to May 2017

require the abandonment of economic truisms we know to be right (free exchange, the merits of improved efficiency, etc.).

To cure this crisis of responsibility, we must resist the urge to apply the victim label and choose to embrace and promote labor market dynamism instead. Only then will we reenergize the virtuous, free market cycle befitting a free and virtuous society.

6

PRO-BUSINESS OR PRO-CRONY

Where Corruption Erodes
Our Cultural DNA

This growing partnership between business and government is a destructive force, undermining not just our economy and our political system, but the very foundation of our culture.

—CHARLES KOCH

In a totalitarian system, social competition manifests itself in the endeavors of people to court the favor of those in power. In the market economy, competition manifests itself in the fact that the sellers must outdo one another by offering better or cheaper goods and services, and that the buyers must outdo one another by offering higher prices.

—LUDWIG VON MISES

I have always considered the biblical passage found in the first book of Samuel, chapter 8, to be the birthplace of statism. We read in this chilling passage of the Israelites being warned that a king would enslave them (v. 11), trample their liberties (12), practice egregious versions of eminent domain (14), and implement a highly confiscatory tax system (15–17). Then in verse 19 we read their reply: "But the people refused to listen to Samuel. They said, 'No, we want a king over us.'"

The people wanted a king. And so the civilizational foundation of statism came to be.

The message to us is profound. Theologically inclined readers can see that the genesis of statism was, first and foremost, idolatry: "And the Lord said, 'It is not you they have rejected, but they have rejected me as their king. As they have done so from the day I brought them out of Egypt until this day, forsaking me and serving other gods" (7–8).

Throughout history, the growth of government has been accompanied by the decline of faithful obedience. Government's ascent to power directly correlated to the people's surrender of moral responsibility. Sure, civil magistrates have been a lot of bad things—abusive, oppressive, redistributionist, tyrannical, arbitrary, self-serving, and corrupt—and more for different peoples at different times since the beginning of civilization. But the people wanted a *king*.

All too often, the prospect of being taken care of, the allure of being led rather than leading, the comfort of having a "savior" has trumped all else, overpowering even the human desire for liberty and flourishing. The record of history is clear as early as the days of the prophet Samuel: when faced with a choice between greater freedom—and the responsibility it requires—or deeper state allegiance, time and again, idolatrous civilizations have chosen the latter.

The choice reveals more about the people than the state. And in this complex reality we uncover one of the key issues dividing conservatives to this day. It's a split I dedicate chapter 10 to exploring, because the divide is all too real. On the one hand, some conservatives believe excessive government results from the greedy state usurping more and more control of the people's lives; on the other hand, others believe it results from the people's ineptness and surrender to the state's overreach.

Both sides are correct, unfortunately. Inadequate *self*-government begins the vicious cycle by creating the need for a more intrusive magistrate, leading to a more dependent people, leading to still greater government, leading to even less self-government, and resulting in even greater state expansion. Rinse and repeat. The consequences include a government payroll of twenty-two million employees and $20 trillion in national debt. It's important to get this cause and effect right, but it's not the subject of this chapter.

Cronyism: Why the People Want a King

We find a disturbing ancient foreshadowing of what plagues us today in the verses prior to the biblical passage I referenced above as the birthplace of statism:

> When Samuel became old, he made his sons judges over Israel. The name of his firstborn son was Joel, and the name of his second, Abijah; they were judges in Beersheba. Yet his sons did not walk in his ways *but turned aside after gain. They took bribes and perverted justice.*
>
> Then all the elders of Israel gathered together and came to Samuel at Ramah and said to him, "Behold, you are old and *your sons do not walk in your ways.* Now appoint for us a king to judge us like all the nations." (1 Samuel 8:1–5, emphasis mine)

Cronyism and corruption caused the people to lose faith and opt for statism. Yes, the people rejected self-government and even theocracy. They were warned of all the consequences for having a king, but they didn't care. They traded the promise of greater freedom and prosperity for a leviathan. But underlying it all, indeed, serving as the impetus to the impulse for big government, was corruption.

Crony capitalism, to use a modern phrase, gave birth to statism. And to be sure, history has done nothing but reinforce this basic reality. Thoughtful people may think it a non sequitur, but it's the way of raw human nature. When we fail to repudiate rent seeking, handouts, sweetheart deals, and the government selecting winners and losers in the marketplace, we risk far more than election results.

Interestingly, the citizens who've rejected elitist forces today have not returned to the miracles of free and open markets, despite holding government and intervening entities in such low regard. How could a society be so displeased with the results of an all-encroaching state and yet *not* demand a renewed love affair with free enterprise to rekindle freedom and prosperity in our society? The answer is tragic: the citizens no longer trust free enterprise to be free at all. They believe it to be a "rigged" game of special favors, handouts, and predetermined advantages for the connected class. Their cynicism isn't entirely justified, but it has enough prima facie support to force proponents of free markets to fight an uphill battle moving forward. That struggle will continue until trust can be reestablished in the public square by demonstrating that the game is not rigged and the government is no longer choosing winners and losers.

Wherever candidates or parties are perceived as cronyist (at the local, state, and federal levels), not only will elections be lost, but truly conservative ideas will fail, as well. When people are forced to choose between what they believe to be a devil they don't trust (corporate interests, Wall Street, big business, greedy developers, etc.) and a devil that at least offers them candy (the blue-state model of big spending, vast government services, and entrenched government programs), they tend to choose the lesser of two evils. At that point, it does no good to argue (correctly, of course) that vast corruption and cronyism also exist behind the second door. We can be right when insisting that the deeply embedded cronyism and corruption of public-employee unions and politicians are no better than crony capitalism—and we'll still lose the argument. Given the choice between the two, *the people want a king.*

The time is now for all who cheer greater individual responsibility and freedom to seize this message. To anyone who thinks the stigma of crony capitalism is *not* election-crushing: ask Hillary Clinton. In spite of having an election matchup that she and the Democratic Party would have gladly moved heaven and earth to create, she lost. She simply could not shake the (accurate) assessment that her Clinton Foundation, corporate speeches, and entire post–White House ecosystem was all one big, crony charade.

To be fair, one could argue that Republicans need this message more, given Donald Trump's populist appeal and electoral success of his promise to "drain the swamp." After the Troubled Asset Relief Program (TARP), Americans felt Wall Street got a crony handout from the Republican Party—an unavoidable outcome of TARP legislation so poorly constructed, executed, administered, and defended in the court of public opinion. Those failures led the American people to hate the "financial bailouts" (a subject for another time), in spite of the fact that Democrats supported the bill. It originated with a Republican president and a Republican treasury secretary. The association between TARP and the GOP was set.

Today, however, at the federal level, the most egregious forms of federal crony capitalism, whether it be the known failure of Solyndra or the perceived success of Tesla, are not associated with the GOP. Republicans must drive this fact home: the Left is using taxpayer dollars to create billionaires. Republicans must advance thoughtful legislation to strip the opportunity for rent seeking from the federal landscape as much as possible.

Needless to say, corporate tax reform is a great place to start. There are numerous ways to strike favoritism and governmental selectivity from the tax code. Proponents of a lower corporate tax rate often correctly applaud the benefit of reestablishing American competitiveness, but the reduction would do much more. Lowering the corporate tax rate would further eliminate the loopholes, deductions, exceptions, and carve-outs that have made such a mockery of the entire revenue-collecting process for American business. Even a low-tax, supply-sider like me believes lowering the rate is only the *second* biggest benefit to be gained. Treating businesses equally under the law—without special regard for influence and power—will prove to have the greatest impact when we flatten the corporate tax code.

What loopholes, you ask? Consider the following exceptions to the tax code for those gifted in the art of influence peddling. These examples leave tax-paying citizens on Main Street shaking their heads at the apparent disparities in the system:

- ▶ A 20 percent tax credit for "qualified research expenses." An actual credit against tax owed for doing what, last I checked, companies are in business to do.
- ▶ The alcohol food credit. We know it in polite society as ethanol. It's a handout to corn producers, pure and simple, and a toxic political issue thanks to Iowa's place as the first caucus state each election season. Rank. Crony. Capitalism.
- ▶ Low-income housing credits for developers. Originally sold as a benefit to the lower-income renters who will eventually inhabit the units, this tax credit not only creates a malignant supply/demand distortion in the marketplace, it also becomes a boondoggle for real estate developers in line for a free-money handout from the taxpayers.

- Accelerated depreciation on machinery and equipment. This tactic simply changes the tax code rules for select industries, period. The change I suggest is not to merely eliminate the accelerated depreciation for the special interests, but to provide instant and full expensing for all sectors. Right now, however, the tax code does a modified version of the right thing for a select group—and excludes all others.
- Film and television production tax credits and rebates. The same films that pay superstar actors and actresses in excess of $20 million for a single movie also receive massive handouts directly from the taxpayers for the privilege of having a film produced in a certain area.
- The entire "qualified production activities" loophole. It's a farce that has always begged for crony exploitation (such as the above film production example). An abstract carve-out that was wrongly designed to serve as a narrow exception for manufacturers became an even worse carve-out when exploited by a plethora of peripheral business sectors.

And those are simply a few of many federal examples. I would need multiple volumes to record examples of cronyism embedded in many city, county, and state tax codes. Sometimes local abuses become national stories, often when involving professional sports stadiums or similar high-profile projects. But even in cases with a smaller profile, city councils and county supervisory boards routinely cut sweetheart deals and use their jurisdiction over zoning laws and entitlements to their benefit. They use local treasury coffers as discretionary slush funds to benefit rich and powerful interests who, not coincidentally, are generous campaign supporters. Corporate special interests are not limited by geography or the size of the jurisdiction.

The conservative reply to the outcry over exceptions to the tax code is often to claim that these companies are merely victims of a punitive tax code. Believe me, I sympathize with their plight. However, cronyism is not the idea of a lower tax burden for all (a concept I vehemently support); cronyism means "lower taxes for me, but not for thee." Cronyism happens when the government uses the tax code to choose which favored activities, sectors, and businesses will receive opportunities for a reduced tax burden, The appropriate conservative policy aspiration—and moral ambition of a good civic society—is a *level playing field*.

At the moment, there is a bipartisan love affair with another prime opportunity for cronyism—infrastructure investment. Yes, there are significant areas of need within our national infrastructure. The majority of these needs reside at local and state levels; however the need for upgrades to various bridges, airports, and tunnels is valid and accepted. But when we hear talk of a "public-private partnership" to meet some of these infrastructure needs, we're hearing an invitation to the worst form of cronyism. Given the bipartisan support for such boondoggles, I can see a lot of it coming down the pike in the next year or so. (Incidentally, it should be no surprise that large developers, construction companies, and engineering firms are often the worst of the crony advocates).

Getting It Right, Right Now

As I said earlier, we must get this message and subsequent policy changes right at the local and state levels to avoid catastrophic results. In city and county politics, concerns over cronyism dominate elections and will dictate the direction of localities for the next generation. Special and targeted incentives are the ultimate slippery slope.

The silly defense I most often hear for government making sweetheart deals with business is that Republicans are supposed to be defenders of business and promoters of growth. Of course, that is correct. However, targeted incentives that favor a particular company or sector fool nobody. They don't promote growth; they reward the powerful who already have the lobbyists, lawyers, and influence to ride the gravy train. Local and state politicians *should* be fostering a pro-business culture—through universally low tax rates for all, not special, lower tax rates for a particular company. They should be lowering regulation, not writing waivers for this or that business.

The Right must be committed to stopping it all, from deplorable stadium deals for billionaire sports team owners to appalling tax favors for connected real-estate developers. Equal opportunity for all means one set of rules for everyone. A city council or a county board defies any reasonable definition of equality under the law when it selectively decides to credit back tax dollars.

There is a concerted effort to manufacture ambiguity about the difference between crony capitalism and legitimate government support for business and growth. Not surprisingly, that ambiguity comes from crony capitalists. Too many Republicans eagerly indict Fannie Mae and Freddie Mac as a perilous example of business and government in bed together; nevertheless, they suddenly become paralyzed with confusion and start babbling about nuance when a big company wants a special tax break to build a new factory or hotel.

To resolve this lack of trust in our cultural institutions, we cannot afford to impose a double standard. We cannot oppose subsidies when we don't like the company, product, or sector in question, but then change our minds when subsidies favor our friends. Likewise, the decision by an employer or a developer to build a project or invest in a community *only* if it receives special treatment is corrupt at its core. Local government can support the free market by not distorting it. City councils should find ways to remove impediments to growth and business for all from their regulatory framework. If they do, they will create fifty times more economic benefit than they could ever do with all the special tax breaks they could ever dream up.

Republicans who believe defeating liberals at the ballot box is our highest ethic (it isn't) must realize the electoral truth. Crony capitalism has been the basis for more Republican election losses in the last forty years than every social issue combined. We can be highly supportive of business and growth in a non-crony way: combine a very low tax base, because of a very nonintrusive government (nonintrusive governments cost less), with very light regulation. Low tax, low regulation—for everyone. It's not complicated.

When these basic right-wing orthodoxies are fairly and consistently upheld, they create even playing fields and promote the dignity of the open marketplace. Whether they're called subsidies, mandates, incentives, or loan guarantees, crony privileges have no place in local, state, or federal politics. It's not only because they make for bad government. They make for a bad society.

This chapter about cronyism belongs in a book about personal responsibility because the perceptions and realities of crony capitalism are helping to disintegrate Main Street's trust in "the system." The underlying message for a path to prosperity is this: we must cultivate and fertilize hard work, innovation, risk taking, and enterprise. Consequently, those people being encouraged to follow that path *must* believe they are operating in a fair environment. The very rich and powerful do not need extra incentives and carve-outs from the tax code to do well. They're almost always extremely capable and resourceful people who need no special advantage. Our founders' vision of "equal under the law" requires a level playing field in the public square and demands the right-sizing of government. Reduce the size of the government engaged in one side of the cronyism and we'll reduce crony capitalism.

The public's faith in the stewardship of the public's assets will only be restored when that faith has been deserved. Without that restored faith, we'll feed the beasts of cynicism and distrust that tear down the norms and conventions vital to a free society. With that rejuvenated faith, we'll enhance the relationship between citizen and state, and feed the engines of entrepreneurial endeavors that create prosperity.

Will people continue to tend to want a king? Sure. But the less corrupt cronyism they see, maybe, just maybe, the less they'll want to choose the leviathan.

7

EMPOWERMENT THROUGH EDUCATIONAL CHOICE
The Great Civil Rights Issue of Our Day

The most promising alternative to top-down efforts to create accountability is school choice. School choice is accountability. When parents have the power to remove their children from a school that is failing them, without financial penalty, not only are they better served, but so is the school they abandon. The threat of losing funds gives failing schools an incentive to improve.

—MICHAEL VAN WINKLE

We have been successful because Americans have known that one's status of birth is not a permanent condition. And your greatest ally in controlling your response to your circumstances has been a quality education. The crisis in K-12 education is a threat to the very fabric of who we are. We have to have high standards for our kids, because self-esteem comes from achievement, not from lax standards and false praise. And we need to give parents greater choice, particularly poor parents whose kids, very often minorities, are trapped in failing neighborhood schools. This is the civil rights issue of our day.

—CONDOLEEZZA RICE

Full disclosure: I attended private faith-based schools with high academic standards throughout my entire K-12 school experience in Orange County, California. I owe a good deal of my intellectual and spiritual development to that experience. Some schools were better than others, but they were all good schools. I felt safe, the teachers cared about the students, and the instruction was both academically rigorous and practical to prepare for life in the real world.

Full confession: I could have never attended these schools based on the economic resources of my family. Were it not for my dad's employment with the school I attended or the assistance he received as a minister and educator in the community, I would have been denied that opportunity.

Now my children all attend high-quality private schools, as well. I am a founder and trustee for a private high school in the affluent community of Newport Beach, California. I'm a highly compensated business owner and professional. I have the disposable income to finance the choice my wife and I have made regarding our children's education. In other words, this chapter about school choice is not about me. As a child, I had a backdoor way into a private education because of my dad's service and, as an adult, I now enjoy the economic resources to make the choices we deem best for our family.

This chapter is also not a creed against public education. Yes, the federalization of public schooling has been an unmitigated disaster. It violates the constitutional role of government and pollutes the proper relationship between states and the federal government in a self-defeating effort that requires localism to succeed. The basic principle of subsidiarity teaches us that highly localized, bottom-up empowered structures will support a more productive, efficient, and desirable outcome. We could introduce other concerns into the conversation, but the societal ill we address in this chapter is not the existence of a highly centralized public school system itself.

Rather, the great civil rights issue of our day is the lack of choice granted to those who need it most, by those who say they believe in choice the most. The incredible irony is that the people most vehemently opposed to choice in education also proudly and emphatically don the pro-choice brand on one particular issue: abortion. The inverse correlation between those who identify as pro-choice (on matters of abortion) and pro-school choice is stunning. But, I digress.

There can be no denial that academic freedom connects directly to the social and cultural "coming apart" that is central to this book. We face a growing gap between different socioeconomic strata, a gap exacerbated by the difference in available educational options. Of course, thousands of public schools are not feeding this great divide, but rather providing stellar educational opportunities to students. But if the greater societal problem is a system often defined by those who think they are on the outside looking in, we have a moral duty not to further handicap those most prone to being "on the outside" by denying them suitable school choice.

A Right View of Education

Before I make the case for greater educational choice in our communities, especially the most disenfranchised ones, I must repudiate a popular leftist belief in direct tension with the view of school choice I propose here. A messianic view of American education has plagued our society for nearly a century—with grave results. We should fight for a productive, safe, and substantive educational experience for every child in a responsible, democratic society—but not because we believe education to be primary to social order or moral formation.

Schooling as a vehicle to teach reading, writing, arithmetic, logic, creativity, comprehension, and critical thinking is at the cornerstone of a proper philosophy of education. Schooling as a *substitute* to family life, religious life, or engagement with community is an abuse of education's intent and proper role. The education process equips a young person to think, to solve problems, and to use resources that will drive their ability to live well. Education is more than the accumulation of facts; therefore, growth during schooling years should be more than merely academic development. Preparing young people to enjoy an abundant life means stimulating intellectual faculties and increasing moral character.

Education is a powerful tool for developing capable and content young people who become flourishing members of society, but it is not the savior for that which plagues humanity. Simply because I rigorously defend school choice for the good of the disenfranchised does not mean I believe education to be society's messiah. Rather, it means I recognize that our present system is experiencing a widening socioeconomic chasm, and the gap in available educational opportunities is contributing to it *significantly*.

Helping Those Who Need It Most

Healthy competition and choice drive better results—it's important to start with this basic normative in a free society. Fear of loss and the negative incentive of losing business or customers don't apply to monopolies and fiefdoms. In the marketplace, no one questions the value to the consumer of choice and competition. However, when it comes to education, bizarre verbal and mental gymnastics are required to deny the value of those same basic principles. Obvious differences between consumer products and education fail to change the fundamental point: when there is no viable alternative to a given school, that school lacks the incentives for efficiency, productivity, and measurable results that it would have if there were healthy competition.

When healthy competition exists for a public school, not only do parents and students who choose a different school benefit (for their own reasons), *but so do the parents and students who choose to stay in the local public school.*

It's an insult to local public schools to claim that school choice offends the legacy of public schools. If they performed well and produced the results desired by their stakeholders (parents, students, and community residents), there would be no assumption that options undermine them. The vast majority of parents want nothing but the best for their children. Sometimes a given family may have a personal reason for wanting children to attend a different school—family dynamics, geography, faith convictions, special needs, sports talents, etc. Other times they may believe their child's unique academic situation calls for a different setting or educational approach. And yes, often the local public school simply fails to deliver the educational results parents wants for their children. Many neighborhood schools simply aren't safe due to crime and drugs.

The reasons could be many—but the fact that a parent would even need to rationalize why they want a certain thing for their child is most peculiar. Since when did we as a society not presume a parent is acting in the best interest of their child? Since when is it the role of a disinterested third party to judge parental rationale for a school decision? From charter schools to private schools, parents might feel a different school is in the best interests of their own family. Are they not entitled to make that choice?

Here is what we do know, courtesy of the nonpartisan Alexander Hamilton Institute.[31] The United States spends over $12,000 per pupil on K-12 public school education. That amount is comparable to the cost of attending many elite private schools. That amount is 30 percent higher than the average cost of primary and secondary education worldwide. And yet, American public school students rank twenty-eighth worldwide in science, thirty-sixth in mathematics, and twenty-fourth in reading. Eighteen countries around the globe outrank American students *in all three categories.*

This macro data in no way condemns all public schools, nor does it vindicate all private schools. It simply establishes the fact that, on a macro level, we have a serious academic proficiency problem—and it's not caused by a lack of funding. And if that *macro* problem exists, it stands to reason that there must be cases on the *micro* level where parental choice seems abundantly warranted.

Critics might claim that using macro data is unfair. What if using national data blends the results of some underfunded states with other states that spend more on education—like California or Illinois—and, therefore, get better results? Perhaps states spending more money are seeing their stellar results hurt in the averages by the underfunded states, the critic might claim. The data tells a different story.

California pays 126.3 percent of the average national teacher's salary, the third highest percentage in the country (behind New York and Massachusetts).[32] Yet California ranks #42 out of the fifty states in the *U.S. News & World Report*'s "Best States for Education, K-12," a ranking based on a composite of test scores and graduation rates. Another prominent study ranks California #40 overall, but #47 in reading and #50 in the pupil-teacher ratio.[33] Is California's education challenge one of funding and financial resources? California spent $76.6 billion on K-12 education in 2015, including federal funds. More than $45 billion from the state general fund (representing more than 40 percent of the state's budget resources) gets spent on K-12 education, with another $15 billion tossed in from local property taxes.[34] Clearly money isn't the problem.

Considering the clout and power of the state's public education union, no one should be surprised at the massive financial resources poured into public education. The California Teachers Association (CTA) boasts a stunning 325,000 members. Their political clout is no small matter, since this one union from one state has "spent more in political campaigning over the last decade than the pharmaceutical industry, oil industry, and tobacco industry—*combined*."[35] Not surprisingly, the CTA has repeatedly defeated various school choice endeavors in the state of California. It successfully prosecuted the passage of Proposition 98, mandating that more than 40 percent of state resources (with annual escalations) be spent on public education (thereby eliminating the opportunity for positive incentives or results-oriented mandates). Teachers are impossible to fire in California (only 0.03 percent are let go after three years on the job).[36] The union has created enough fiscal insanity to warrant its own book, but it's their detrimental actions toward students that is most disturbing.

But, one might counter, what if a parent happens to be unconcerned about the data points I've shared or the widely disseminated school rankings? Indeed, many California parents and students have a wonderful school and school district and wouldn't want to change schools. Great! That's a rather obvious beauty of *choice*—they are free to choose to stay right where they are! But all taxpayers pay into the education system. In those instances where a parent feels the need for a different educational option for their own kids, why shouldn't they have the freedom to choose the best opportunity as they see it?

No one is suggesting states pay more for that parental choice than they are already paying for every other student. School choice need not, and should not, cost the state more. Nor am I suggesting that a voucher or credit should be made available for families like mine who have the financial means to fund their own education choices.

There is, however, a belief implied in the rejection of school choice for lower- and middle-income families. It is the same belief driving the present state of cultural angst: *lower- and middle-income families do not deserve the same educational opportunities that higher-income families have, nor do they want them.* It is the textbook definition of elitism—the belief that people on the bottom half of the economic strata are intellectually inferior. This has caused much of the resentment and alienation we see in culture today.

In the face of such elitism, school choice proponents know there is overwhelming evidence that many students and families of lesser means earnestly desire to learn and crave greater educational opportunity. Time and time again, the ability to cross-pollinate wealthier, bright students with lower-income and middle-income bright students results in an economically agnostic result. All students have thrived together in such a scenario with no regard for the financial status of one student over another. Why then are private schools often perceived as exclusive dens for the elite? Because the lack of school choice has guaranteed it to be so! Introducing school choice alternatives would compress that economic delta and provide opportunities, where parents deem it necessary, for those who need it most.

Tax Credits and Vouchers

I'm not one to shy away from a granular policy debate about school choice, because details do matter. Many states and individual districts have performed well with robust charter initiatives allowing expanded educational options. "Trigger laws" have enabled parents to convert schools deemed to be failing into an independent charter model. Although cherry-picked cases of poorly performing charter schools can be found, the positive data points provide a stark contrast to the alternative. When it comes right down to it, a child attending a charter school represents a *choice* made by stakeholders, parents exercising their moral authority as parents.

Charter schools are funded by the massive resources of the tri-funded school districts (local property tax receipts, state funding, and federal budget disbursements). But another tool for providing greater academic freedom is the use of tax credits and tax vouchers. I favor tax credits because the funds pass directly from the state to the taxpayer, not from the state to the school. While a tax voucher program would vastly improve the present lack of choice, it could also push the state down a slippery slope. We'd end up with the same problem we have now if the state believed the funding subsidy empowered its bureaucracy to make various management decisions, such as curriculum, agenda, or personnel.

History has already demonstrated this to be a valid concern. In states where voucher programs exist, we have seen a small but greater likelihood for increased regulatory burden, whereas states where tax credit programs exist have been virtually free from such interventions.[37] Tax credits have been deemed fully constitutional and offer a tested program that avoids government interference while opening educational opportunities to all families and students.

Where the Need Is Greatest

I call school choice a civil rights issue because the sociological data demonstrates that higher concentrations of minority students, particularly Hispanics and African-Americans, are forced to attend underperforming schools. Successful, well-educated families contributing to society, putting their kids in great schools, and seeing those kids become successful, well-educated members of society is a self-fulfilling prophecy. But it should not be a process monopolized by the rich and elite. Through school choice, families who have known adversity and impoverishment can access extraordinary educational opportunity. School choice directly impacts minority and working-class white neighborhoods where the need is clearly greatest.

School choice keeps the education of our kids local, as it should be. School choice empowers parents to make a change. Parents who fear humanistic indoctrination, failing high-crime schools, or standards imposed by bureaucrats in Washington, DC, can make a change—for the good of their children. If school choice were to become the battle cry of the present populist rage, we would see a truly righteous transformation. Instead of chasing alleged bogeymen such as Goldman Sachs or a Chinese trade pact, we could end the lack of policy innovation in education and do good for many who are truly disenfranchised.

Education is not our messiah. Education is *a* building block of our society, not the complete building or even its foundation. Expanding educational opportunity makes it possible to reverse course, but by no means guarantees it. Nevertheless, those who care for the forgotten men and women in our society should embrace school choice as among the lowest hanging fruit imaginable, the easiest way to dramatically improve their opportunities for success in our new global economy. When we see educational opportunity improve, we will see the disenfranchised empowered in ways never imagined by the social warriors of our time.

8

WHERE CULTURE TRUMPS GREEN CARD

Patriotism, Immigration, and Nationalism

Our patriotic fervor was the result of the old and widespread belief in the idea of American exceptionalism, the idea that America was a new thing in history, different from other countries. Other nations had evolved one way or another: evolved from tribes, from a gathering of the clans, from inevitabilities of language and tradition and geography. But America was born, and born of ideas: that all men are created equal, that they have been given by God certain rights that can be taken from them by no man, and that those rights combine to create a thing called freedom.

—PEGGY NOONAN

Democracy, immigration, multiculturalism—pick any two!

—JAMES C. BENNETT

I cannot imagine a more divisive and controversial issue in the present political spectrum than immigration. It divides the Left and the Right—and thus the two major political parties— and frankly, it splits *the conservative Right*, as well.

Many people had significant concerns about illegal immigration long before 9/11, primarily in southern border states where cheap labor from immigration was perceived as having a negative impact on the economy. Over the years, the primary driver of illegal immigration angst has shifted on occasion—national security concerns, economic fairness, and concerns about drugs and gang violence. Regardless of the driver, it has remained a politically toxic issue. Not being perceived as "tough" on immigration has been lethal for Republican candidates in the last two election cycles. On the other hand, taking the lead as the hawkish anti-illegal immigration advocate became political gold for candidate Trump, particularly in the Republican primary.

It can be challenging to sort through the varying viewpoints on the subject because many outspoken voices share the same conclusions, but for completely different reasons. The American tradition has certainly been pro-immigration. Thus, to associate pro-immigration sentiments with a form of anti-patriotism is either misguided or could be a reflection of a significant shift in circumstances. It is futile to evaluate the immigration conversation in a vacuum, divorced from broader concerns about economic nationalism, labor protectionism, national security, the rule of law, and—the most controversial of subjects—multiculturalism.

There is no point in bemoaning the political heat that exists around immigration. I spoke to Gov. Rick Perry at a private dinner in New York City, in January 2015. I asked about his messaging strategy for a nuanced view on immigration in the pending political season. His take was that the issue had calmed down. The public was ready for a more palatable policy response that included a little bit of discourse and a lot of understanding. He ended up being one of the first candidates to drop out of the race, despite being one of the most qualified and recognizable.

Governor Perry can be forgiven for overestimating the public's patience. He was not alone. By late 2015, it was abundantly clear that much of the public believed illegal immigration to be...

- ▶ a risk to national security
- ▶ the source of economic angst for the labor force's lower end of wage earners
- ▶ a threat to America's identity and culture
- ▶ or a combination of two or all of the above statements

The general distrust each side has for one another has made it even more difficult to work through the complexity of the issue. If one side questions the wisdom of not enforcing present immigration law, they're often assumed to be xenophobic or even racist. On the other hand, if one side favors an easier *legal* immigration process and questions the wisdom or practicality of deporting fifteen million people, they're accused of being anti-American or opposed to the rule of law. We're not going to achieve clarity without a commitment to more charitable discourse about our legitimate disagreements, sans toxic rhetoric and accusations.

I address the topic of immigration here in this book on our cultural addiction to blame because illegal immigration is often accused of contributing to the economic plight of the American worker. Just as we evaluated economic reality and the logic involved in the difficulties with free trade and automation in chapter 5, we will do the same here with a candid look at the economic reality and logic of immigration and labor.

The Economic Mythology of Illegal Immigration

There is a plethora of reasons to desire strong borders, chief among them being national security. However, my thesis is simple: the notion that hardworking American citizens are being denied a chance to make an honest wage by illegal immigrants is economic mythology.

Furthermore, it is multiculturalism, not illegal immigration, that has altered the national immigration conversation from the days when the tired and weary flocked to Ellis Island, "yearning to be free." Our patriotic and proud American identity is threatened now, not because white Americans need protection from cheaper labor. It is threatened by a hideous multiculturalism, incompatible with American ideals, that has snuffed out our once proud understanding of the distinctive and exceptional American experiment.

I confess that this chapter has little chance of not bothering someone, due to the aforementioned polarization. Yet this issue begs for thoughtful people to carefully consider both premises and conclusions in a nuanced way. I have certain conclusion sympathies with some people, and yet have little sympathy for how they got there. We must consider national security concerns, both from jihadist enemies and violent gang or drug trafficking criminals. Yet legitimate national security concerns are sometimes clouded by bogus economic concerns. My sincere hope is that this chapter will take the high road in the conversation, offering a way to think about this issue that respects rule of law, seeks an appropriate public policy resolution, prevents scapegoating, and, most importantly, reframes the conversation around values identity, with an eye toward sincere patriotism, not mere labor protectionism.

Multinational immigration in the days of Ellis Island was, indeed, a hallmark of American history. It spoke to what was special about the United States of America—people wanted to come here from all over the world, because they desired a better life for themselves and their families. The country's national character, her free enterprise economy, her religious freedom, and her opportunity society were the envy of the world—and for good reason. The nation not only had plenty of room for the immigrants, she benefitted tremendously from the increased population so pivotal to economic growth. The economy needed more producers and consumers—it got both from a multiplicity of countries. And while the immigration was multi-continental, a heavy volume of immigrants came across from the European continent.

The difference between what drove immigration then and now is key to our national discussion. America's free enterprise system drew people here 125 years ago. Too often today, our welfare state and public entitlements act as immigration magnets. I say "too often," because it would be too broad of a generalization to suggest they are the exclusive magnets today. Well-intentioned people who desperately want to create a better life for their families frequently cross the U.S. southern border. They come prepared to work hard to earn a living and care for their families, including other generations and family extensions in Mexico or Central America. I do not condone their illegal entry, but how we approach the immigration of a hardworking, devoted family man should differ from how we view the grifter looking to exploit America's social safety net.

I know a great deal of Hispanic immigrants want to flee poverty. Nevertheless, the abuse of our welfare state by illegal immigrants has infuriated the American people and done irreparable harm to a liberal immigration framework. Living off the public dole never occurred to the Ellis Island immigrant, while many twenty-first-century, southern border immigrants happily take the handouts of benefits. This reality is more a critique of our welfare state than of immigration itself, but I have to accept that the two cannot be divorced in this dialogue any longer. However, the most problematic aspect of the situation today is not the generous entitlements often received by immigrants.

Multiethnic, Not Multicultural

Ellis Island immigration was multinational, but committed to assimilation. Not so today. In fact, the polar opposite is true. Our societal commitment to a squishy form of multiculturalism accompanies much of today's immigration. Consequently, immigrants are no longer expected to learn the language, know the history, understand our civic life, or appreciate national unity. Long gone is the day when immigration implied entering into the American social contract with a solidly American foundation.

America's immigration heritage is indeed multiethnic, but not multicultural. It was, in fact, *proudly* multiethnic, but it was also *proudly* committed to *Americanization*. Our culture's family structure, national language, and proud civic heritage were all natural expectations for the immigrants of past generations. There were no controversies about whether or not students would learn and recite the pledge of allegiance to our flag in class. No one debated whether the American national anthem could be played at a sports game without offending attendees. These were cultural *givens*.

The breakdown of this cultural context is the real reason the subject of immigration has gone nuclear. Fusing intense multiculturalism with liberal immigration created the unworkable situation we now have today. The model of assimilation we enjoyed for so long in America shaped a successful immigration history. Pride in ethnic heritage was never discouraged, as evidenced by ethnic celebrations of customs, food, music, and even holidays. As James Bennett said, "Ethnicity was a sort of style rather than fundamental identity."

I go to great lengths to clarify the three points that follow because they're crucially important to my own ideology, and I earnestly desire to maintain your ear for a final point I must make (one sure to ruffle radical isolationists).

In a post-9/11 world, we have every right and every responsibility to vigorously defend ourselves, to keep out those who want to get in to harm our country. In this sense, I vehemently support the national defense objective of a hawkish immigration policy, carefully vetting those who would enter.

For those who desire to enter American society, the goal of creating a better life for themselves and their families is a noble one. Their ingenuity, work ethic, and productivity should be encouraged and embraced. However, the idea of making our entitlement systems available to noncitizens should be vehemently rejected and, until it can be rejected, should significantly inform our national immigration policy.

If America is to maintain an immigration invitation, she must restore a culture of assimilation that prizes America's heritage, ideas, ideals, and values. Our national and cultural distinctions should not and cannot be denigrated or negotiated away. Our departure from successful immigration precedent caused much of the angst and even toxicity we face on the subject now.

With this healthy, balanced, and nuanced firmly laid, what room is there, if any, for the disgruntled American worker to blame immigrants from the south for their economic plight today? Has there been an "invasion from the south" responsible for "taking their jobs"? Did low-cost Hispanic labor replace American factory workers in Buffalo, New York, or Aliquippa, Pennsylvania? What do sound economic principles say? Or has this issue been used to feed our cultural addiction to blame, further exacerbating our crisis of responsibility?

Economic Absurdities of the Southern "Invasion"

It is anti-American and anti–free enterprise—the idea that any individual or group should be protected from those willing to work at a lower cost. This chapter will never end if I must qualify every statement I make with the three points I emphatically summarized above. I'm not defending the aspects of this issue that I've already condemned. I am trying to purposely *isolate* the economic aspect of the subject. In what way, in and of itself, is a lower-cost worker a "threat" to another or an "invasion" of some sort?

If you separate the question from the toxicity of the current debates, it becomes an absurd proposition. No one would ever try to protect a Stanford computer science PhD from an invasion of lower-cost programmers from India. No one would claim a real estate broker working for 2 percent commission to be an affront to the long-established broker in town who has always charged 3 percent. Negotiation over the cost of labor is as American as, well, negotiating over the cost of *anything*. It is at the heart of a free enterprise society. The mere willingness to do work at a lower cost does not represent an ipso facto offense.

The law of comparative advantage is in play here. Our economy becomes more productive when we have more customers to sell to. When many jobs for low-skilled laborers are filled, the opportunity moves upstream where more skills and experience (and therefore higher wages) can be utilized. Immigration creates a higher supply of workers while simultaneously creating higher demand. That truth is an economic given that cannot be disputed without overturning basic conventional economic orthodoxies.

The supply of workers allegedly diluting the labor pool also buy food, shop at the mall, seek shelter, and otherwise stir the invisible hand of the marketplace. This expanded need in the economy creates a greater need for labor to serve it. Plus, if immigrant labor finds itself on the lowest end of the wage spectrum, it provides greater opportunity for somewhat higher wage labor elsewhere. To deny this is to imply that the smallest countries should be the richest ones, and the largest countries the poorest ones. But of course, the opposite is true.

The reality is that in economic booms and economic contractions we have a long history of low-skill labor shortages. Often immigrants did the work no one else could be found to do. Many who bemoan the economic impact of immigrants do not intend to direct their fire at the job demand itself, but on the wages that go with the jobs. In other words, they advocate for economic protectionism.

But all serious study of this issue has shown that areas with high immigration show no statistically material difference from areas with low or no immigration when it comes to wage impact. In fact, an analysis of immigration's impact on the wages of American natives with comparable educations suggests an effect of no more than 0.4 percent over a twenty-year period.[38] In addition, the employment rates for immigrants and native-born Americans move in nearly perfect tandem with one another, disputing the idea of one camp taking "market share" from the other.[39] To the extent that we saw greater labor success for immigrants versus natives after the 2008 financial crisis (both disputable and infinitesimal), it can be traced entirely to mobility. Immigrants were simply more willing to move in response to the changing local labor markets.

American immigration is pivotally important to our long-term economic health. I say that with the aforementioned principles and commitments firmly in mind. For example, high-skilled immigrants have become vital to our economy for their contributions to technology innovation. The labor force of our country has faced a secular decline, led by the social deterioration we talked about in chapter 3, and by shifting demographics that have worked against the active labor force (baby boomers retiring, etc.). Immigration represents an important feed of needed supply into the labor force, not to mention to the national customer base. We need population growth for economic growth. The ideas, labor, and commerce that come from increased immigration are not merely good, but required for continued economic health.

There can be no perfect equilibrium on this immigration issue. Yes, there are certainly situations in which a competitive immigrant worker who is in the country illegally displaces an American worker. It is totally unnecessary to the broader points I am making to deny that reality. My intent is not to minimize or trivialize those situations. Rather, it is to demonstrate that such a problem is not systemic and cannot be the final point in the conversation. Only a crisis of responsibility would allow a worker to conclude that *there are less educated, less capable workers of another ethnicity doing work for less than what I would like to be paid, so I give up.* And, of course, most Americans would never say as much.

Perhaps if the three points I laid out as foundational to this complex subject were in place, the discussion of immigration's impact on labor markets and wages would be moot. I suspect that to be the case. My skepticism that the American worker is being economically assaulted by immigration does not dilute my impassioned plea for a sensible national security solution for immigration, the elimination of magnetic welfare benefits for immigrants, or a return to American assimilation as fundamental to the immigration process.

Regardless of the exact plight any American worker experiences as this complicated immigration subject works itself out, the basic principles of rugged individualism must drive our thinking. No worker is entitled to a given wage. Our society desperately needs a return to the rule of law. Our immigration policies require a thoughtful and comprehensive redo that will reinforce the greater good of American civic life. Self-refuting and futile economic protectionism need not play a role.

Yes, the "establishment" needs to get the policy paradigm right on this complex and multilayered subject. But there is no magic panacea to be found for the American worker. Eliminating the immigrant labor pool will not solve our deficiencies regarding mobility, individualism, and cultural commitment to work. In fact, doing so would simply shrink the aggregate demand in the economy and further diminish the very healthy competition that drives productivity.

Only a crisis of responsibility could assert that what is keeping the native working class from a chance at success is the presence of mostly unskilled and uneducated laborers. It is not true. We know it from a study of the data and, if we are being honest, from our own intuition, as well.

Our cultural crisis of responsibility gets no waiver from the immigration issue.

9

HIGHER EDUCATION'S
SAFE SPACES

Kerosene on the Crisis

A university is not a political party, and an education is not an indoctrination.

—DAVID HOROWITZ

Campuses are bubbles, artificial environments that insulate students from the life of the competitive marketplace. The more exact truth is that our campuses offer students the privileges of liberty without the corresponding responsibilities.

—PETER AUGUSTINE LAWLER

If the path to a free and virtuous society must go through collegiate academia, our quest to restore responsibility is going to be a rough and tumble ride. As I've already argued for the importance of labor dynamism and educational choice, clearly the path must take us through the "safe spaces" that our colleges and universities have become. The only question is how things might look as students emerge on the other side.

We have a major problem in this country if we aspire to a culture rooted in responsibility, accountability, and free and independent thinking—higher education is pouring kerosene on the fire that is our economic, moral, and cultural crisis. It's a multipronged problem. Higher education has damaged the very concept of responsibility and facilitated economic irresponsibility by encouraging a student debt system that has exceeded any notion of common sense. It has engendered resentment in so many millennials who were sold a bill of goods about the value of a college degree in their portfolio. By promoting relativism on college campuses, the higher education industry has wreaked havoc on the basic definition, if not the very existence, of values, character, and responsibility.

I vacillate between two distinct schools of thought in the world of higher education critics. I find common cause with both and do not see them as mutually exclusive. One approach emphasizes the ghastly fiscal recklessness of the present system that creates an incredible gap between reality and expectation for anyone receiving an undergraduate college degree from a university *not* considered one of the elite twenty-five schools. The other approach laments the extremely radical indoctrination of students into secular humanism being presented as common fare. The truth about the sad state of higher education is not *either/or* but *both/and*.

The American university system now offers families the worst of both worlds—inherit insane debt and receive little preparation for adult responsibilities, while being indoctrinated with propositions that undermine the foundational values of Western civilization. That's right. One can now go broke being taught to think incorrectly.

Truth be told, my two major categories of concern in academia (economic and ideological) have been overshadowed in recent years by a third. The infantilizing of young adults on campus—the "snowflake factor"—represents the worst of our present crisis of responsibility.

Much has been made of "safe spaces" on college campuses and the extent to which universities are going to make sure students are never offended, challenged, or intellectually stimulated. Fear of offense is a one-way street, of course. Christian and politically conservative students routinely face harassment and belligerent hostility while being made the pariahs of university life. Cable news overflows with stories of conservative speakers being uninvited, harassed, or threatened. In several cases, full-blown riots have met respected, conservative intellectuals invited to address a student club or organization. Academic censorship is problematic enough, and antithetical to the very cause of higher education just one generation ago. But the real cause for concern is the objective behind it: *the belief that young adults need to be protected from anything and everything that causes them discomfort.*

If a "religion of irresponsibility" is taking hold in our culture today, our college campuses serve as that religion's church. Basic adult characteristics of resilience, patience, tolerance, respect, humility, acceptance, inquiry, and discovery—all have been sacrificed at the altar of the "snowflake factor." My agenda is to repudiate the victimhood culture at all levels, especially in the college years where it is programmed into the minds and hearts of our young people. The good intentions behind these efforts, if any exist, are no good to us. The very vernacular being used— microaggressions, safe spaces, and trigger warnings—form an easy bridge into a life of victimhood.

What's the best way to reprogram the message that you're entitled to never hear contrary opinions? Real life. This book is about seeing a *better real life* for the millions of Americans feeling left out of that possibility. Our colleges are programming fragility, when they should be programming the opposite. Fragility is the enemy of a good life.

The Good Old College Lie

It's not my intent merely to oppose the coddling of young adults (though I surely do). The snowflake factor is but one of three major categories of cultural challenges stemming from higher education. It is a self-reinforcing one, however, because when people encounter real-life problems—after being convinced they had a right to live offense-free—they tend to fall deeper into the woes of victimhood. Unfortunately, those who embrace victimhood inevitably find ways to remain a victim. But if we eliminated the snowflake charade tomorrow in its entirety, we'd still be left with a failing ideological framework and a university business model that would be laughable if it weren't so fatal.

There's no mystery as to the source of angst for young college graduates in this new economy. Consider the following data points that make the case succinctly and dramatically:[40]

- In the last ten years alone, total student debt has risen 250 percent.
- Cumulative student loan debt now exceeds $1.4 trillion, greater than total national credit card debt and the total national mortgage debt—by a wide margin.
- In the last ten years, the number of borrowers has increased 90 percent.
- The average balance size has increased by 80 percent.
- Roughly $1 trillion of new student loan debt has been added in just the last decade.

These stunning figures coincide with the most difficult environment for young adults to find a livable wage in seventy-five years. They coincide with the highest percentage of young adults moving back in with their parents in seventy-five years. How bad is that reality? The percentage of twenty-five- to thirty-five-year-olds living with their parents is *double what it was in 1964*. Double!

And it's 33 percent higher than at the turn of the millennium.[41] It's interesting to note: as the unemployment rate for this age demographic was cut in half from 2010–2016, the percentage of those living at home increased 25 percent.[42] This inverse correlation suggests that either new jobs don't pay enough or perpetual adolescence has become the new normal.

And is it mere coincidence that five pivotal swing states in the 2016 election where so much middle-class angst resides— Michigan, Iowa, Wisconsin, Ohio, and Pennsylvania—are in the top sixteen for debt per student?[43]

What's driving this explosion of student debt? Primarily, increased college expense is to blame. Why the stratospheric increase in the cost of college? The subsidy created by the easy availability of debt. Consequently, the vicious cycle damages the very people it was supposed to benefit. A college degree was portrayed as a key asset for young people looking to climb the socioeconomic ladder. Nearly infinite student loans were then made available so more people could have this key asset. The high demand coupled with infinite government loans gave universities free reign to raise tuition. And so it goes. As a result, college expenses skyrocketed many multiples higher than the base inflation rate, university administrator and bureaucrat salaries began to resemble those of elite CEOs, and average college graduate wages declined by 15 percent.[44]

These underperforming, overvalued colleges feed the students' sense of entitlement. Perhaps students would tolerate being roughed up a bit academically if they weren't required to pay in excess of $250,000 to be there!

Who's to blame for this mess? There's plenty of blame to go around—from the obnoxious federal loan subsidies that drive prices higher and indebt our young people at torturous levels, to the administrators and boards that have lost any concept of fiduciary duty to those they are supposed to educate. Let's not forget the parents who enabled this national charade, perhaps to preserve their own pride.

And universities don't have to deal with the market force that would usually drive prices down—competition. Schools know every kid arrives with a government-backed checkbook; therefore, instead of focusing on academic rigor at competitive pricing, they focus on amenities and wasteful spending projects they think will make their school a student magnet.

Young people are disgruntled today because they were sold a lie—*a four-year degree will guarantee economic security*. While that may have been true to some extent in the past, it changed when the university ceased to be a place for intellectual growth and increased productivity. A classically liberal education—one that better prepares the student for real life, stimulates their passions, and encourages them to wrestle with the great questions of life—has gone the way of the Hula-Hoop (and, coincidentally, the decline began around the same decade as the Hula-Hoop). As Charles Murray points out, there is still a compensation premium for college graduates over non-college graduates. The big question is *why*? It most certainly cannot and will not last.

The monumental debt, and poor rationale for its existence, is made exponentially worse by the poor quality of the product itself. In his masterful work *Fail U: The False Promise of Higher Education*,[45] Charlie Sykes meticulously walks readers through the decline in rigor, academic quality, and faculty—or teachers who even show up for class. Two courses a semester is considered an above-average teaching load now for a college professor (roughly five hours per week). Although based on the steady flow of horror stories about what gets taught when professors do show up, I suppose there's something to be said for the absentee model of teacher aide-driven education. The only thing worse than a radical teacher being paid well not to teach is a radical teacher being paid well to teach humanistic extremism.

Rethinking College

Our pursuit of a free and virtuous society finds a significant obstacle in this higher education crisis. What's at stake is that pivotal period in a young life where many are intellectually curious, craving new experiences, and dabbling with social freedom for the first time. Noble aims of a college-age experience should include developing marketable job skills, enhancing one's ability to think critically, and discovering where one's real passions and aspirations lie. Instead, academia insists on protecting its monopoly, as evidenced by tyrannical opposition to trade schools and technology-driven distance learning.

Sadly, only one option remains to remove the present monopoly controlled by ideological leftists who coddle young adults—*blow up the business model*. With student debt growing exponentially, some form of dramatic default may be required to force stakeholders in the present system to make changes.

In the meantime, each family has every right and responsibility to evaluate its own situation and conduct an analysis of costs versus benefits. Is rigorous worldview training in matters of life and philosophy the primary objective? Perhaps a smaller private or faith-based college is the right path. Does the prospective student have a clear idea of what they want to do professionally, where a trade school or niche training may be more valuable to achieve their underlying objective? Is the primary objective to gain the life experiences of the college years? If so, does everyone understand the debt ramifications and what post-college life might look like?

In other words, there is no one-size-fits-all solution for each family and young adult. In an era where free trade and immigration are often blamed for the entire plight of middle America, what we know is that skyrocketing college costs (completely separated from monetary or market conditions) have left an entire class of people unable to receive a college education. And those who do have access to it and incur the debt to get it are flat-out not receiving it. Instead, they're incurring a quarter-million dollars of debt for a pat-on-the-back and a declining wage. Meanwhile, the true traits that lead to prosperity—character development, problem solving, resilience, and mature interpersonal skills—are ignored or shunned.

The way forward begins with a renewed care for independent thinking. It starts with a genuine appreciation for the dignity of the individual as a person, not merely as a potential loan customer. It continues with letting technological innovations enter (and even disrupt) higher education. And it includes hitting the reset button on our culture's attitude toward college.

Purging a broken business model from the system will be hard enough; purging extremism and hostile ideology will be even harder. But, ultimately, the stakes are too high to ignore the damage being done by the present system. The cause of a free and virtuous society requires the courage to take this head-on.

10

GOVERNMENT BY THE PEOPLE, FOR THE PEOPLE

Why the Stunning Incompetence and Inefficiency of Big Government Is the People's Problem

There are always those who are willing to surrender local self-government and turn over their affairs to some national authority in exchange for a payment of money out of the Federal Treasury. Whenever they find some abuse needs correction in their neighborhood, instead of applying the remedy themselves they seek to have a tribunal sent on from Washington to discharge their duties for them, regardless of the fact that in accepting such supervision they are bartering away their freedom.

—PRESIDENT CALVIN COOLIDGE

Let us never forget that government is ourselves and not an alien power over us. The ultimate rulers of our democracy are not a president and senators and congressmen and government officials, but the voters of this country.

—PRESIDENT FRANKLIN D. ROOSEVELT

Only a virtuous people are capable of freedom. As nations become corrupt and vicious, they have more need of masters.

—BENJAMIN FRANKLIN

I referenced author J. D. Vance's bestselling memoir *Hillbilly Elegy* in chapter 3. Its underlying plea is for conservatives to quit telling poor white America that government caused their plight. When I was growing up, I had always associated victimhood with the Left. It seemed to me that those blaming some force, entity, or movement for suppressing or preventing them from being their best selves were always on the political Left.

However, the cultural addiction to blame I have focused on throughout this book has covered all comers, the usual bogeymen of both the Left and the Right. Unfortunately, championing victimhood has now become a bipartisan affair, although the identity of the targets shifts depending on one's political party or ideology. Right-wing circles do have peripheral culprits for the plight of man (e.g., the Federal Reserve, labor unions, an overreaching judiciary), but the overarching villain in almost any right-wing narrative about the ills of society is the government—usually the federal government.

Hence, it is my burden in this chapter to plead with my right-wing brethren to see big government for what it is: *the consequence—and not the cause—of our problems.*

The foundation of conservative ideology is, indeed, limited government. The contemporary Left either forgets or dismisses the fact that our nation's founders shared this vision. The founders' genius was not to create a deliberately weak or an abundantly strong government, but rather to subject the government's powers to checks and balances. They first acknowledged as core to our nation's own soul that "governments are instituted among men, deriving their just powers from the consent of the governed." They rooted the American experiment in the belief that government does not grant rights to man, but rather, man grants government its limited power. Man enjoys certain natural rights and forms governments to help secure those rights.

The founders did not distrust government or suffer from some sort of government-abuse hangover merely as a reaction to the tyranny of King George III. Rather, America is an idea, a manifestation of a world-changing philosophical view—sovereignty belongs to the people alone. Not a monarch, not a feudal class, not a hereditary class—but to the people. It only makes sense that a society built around the idea of the state would grant the state unlimited power, but a society built around the natural and universal rights of humanity would limit the state's power only to what is needed to secure those rights.

Conservatives, at least as I use the term, seek to *conserve* this people-centered philosophy at the root of our nation's founding. The founders envisioned a government held in check by its own constitutional limitations; thus, those who value conserving this philosophy today should share that political intuition.

There are three primary structural forms for those constitutional limitations: (1) the checks and balances embedded in the three-branch system of government; (2) the enumeration of their powers in the Constitution; and (3) the delegation of powers to the individual states wherever powers were not specifically delegated to the federal government in the Constitution. To reiterate, the genius of the founders was both philosophical and administrative. It reflected their view of human nature, of natural law, and of natural rights; and it protected the people from abuses and overreach through procedural design.

And all of it—all of it—depended on *moral* and *responsible* citizens.

The Behemoth of Federal Government

Any two conservatives are very likely to agree that a large and centrist federal government is outside the design of our country's heritage. Where they may disagree is whether big government was the result of *government taking* on an excessive load (usurping), or the result of the *people giving* them an excessive load (dereliction of duty). Let's start with a fact about which both sides of this debate can agree: the federal government is a monstrosity.

As I mentioned earlier, one of my favorite things to do in Washington, DC, is to look out the windows at the top of the Washington Monument on each side (north, south, east, west). The caretakers of this national treasure provide visitors with a sort of "visual progression," showing visitors decades of photographs to demonstrate how the view has changed over time. In each direction, visitors see a visual memorial of the growth of government, as plethora of federal government buildings, branches, offices, and infrastructure sprout up year after year, decade after decade.

Unlike the growth of a successful corporation, the buildup of government facilities hasn't been accompanied by greater results, better fiscal management, increased efficiency, or a more robust civic life. Rather, each additional bureaucratic layer brings more debt, dysfunction, and angst. Federal budget outlays were only $68 billion in 1952. They grew to $660 billion per year in 1981, and are now barely below $3.8 trillion per year (fig. 10.1).

FIGURE 10.1

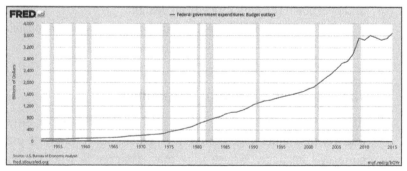

Employees of government (federal, state, and local) now total over 22 million people. In a labor force estimated to be 160 million people, 14 percent of our workforce is employed by the government (fig. 10.2).

Not surprisingly, fiscal conservatives bemoan our incomprehensible level of debt—about $20 trillion on our national credit card. Annual budget deficits between $400 billion and $1 trillion (each of the last ten years) intensify the fears of budget hawks. But perhaps most concerning is the percentage of the economy that federal spending now represents—fully 24 percent of national GDP (fig. 10.3). Federal spending has essentially doubled its role in the economy since the 1950s —even while the economy was dramatically expanding most of that time.

Economists refer to this concern as the "crowding out" effect. It doesn't require an economic textbook to understand. The government doesn't make anything, produce anything, sell anything, or engage in any rational economic behavior. In fact, by definition, any dollar it spends is either a dollar it took from the private economy via confiscatory taxation, or a dollar it borrowed and will have to be paid back by taxpayers. Consequently, the more dollars coming from government spending, the fewer dollars available for more productive purposes in the economy.

Two things must be said about this reality, and each will likely irritate one side of the aisle or the other. First, simply because government spending is "unproductive" in an economic sense does not mean it is illegitimate. Government has a legitimate function, and those functions have to be paid for. Second, to deny that money gets used more productively in the private economy is to deny the fundamental tenets of free enterprise and the profit motive.

The percentage of the economy being encapsulated by government spending is a huge concern for many reasons. For example, military spending as a percentage of the economy has

FIGURE 10.2

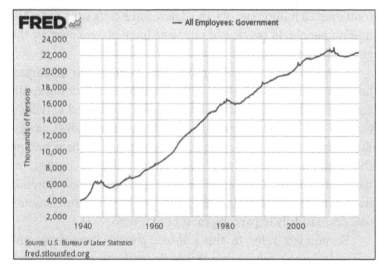

FIGURE 10.3

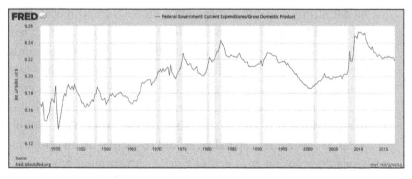

shrunk rapidly since the 1950s. We saw a temporary increase in the 1980s for the Cold War and in the 2000s for the two wars in the Middle East. But the *percentage* of government spending has stayed below half of its previous levels, even with those two periods. Right now it is only one-third of those prior levels. How has government spending exploded as a percentage of the economy while the military spending portion of our economy has been dramatically reduced?

The answer is the increase in transfer payments. In fact, if we spent no money on anything but transfer payments, we would still run a deficit in this country. If we had no governmental departments, no salaries, no military, no debt interest, no programs—just Medicare, Medicaid, Social Security, Welfare, Unemployment, and so on.—we would still be in a financial hole (fig. 10.4).

There can be legitimate discussions around what has been acceptable government expansion and what has not. But taken in a macro sense, our government has grown beyond anyone's comprehension in the last fifty years, and conservatives, at least, are frustrated by the inefficiency, bureaucracy, and staggering

FIGURE 10.4

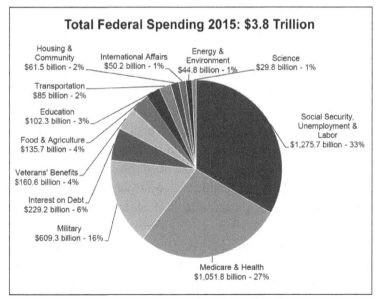

*National Priorities Project, Federal Spending: Where does the money go, 2015

fiscal implications. I am on the list of those frustrated by the inefficiency, bureaucracy, and fiscal implications, but none of those things sit atop my list of concerns with bigger government.

What Should Bother Us Most

The vast majority of the conservative Right directs its ire at the unsustainable debt and entitlement trajectory (at least it did during the Obama years). The big government spending and deficits beginning with the Bush presidency and continuing into the Obama presidency gave birth to the Tea Party movement, which focused on the need for fiscal responsibility. As I said, I agree that to leave our children and grandchildren this kind of debt is a dereliction of duty. But alas, neither the expansive bureaucracy nor the fiscal recklessness of government is the cause of my most intense ire. If some sort of private sector "sugar daddy" paid off our national debt, I do not believe we should be happy in any way, shape, or form. Here's why: The size of government is not the cause of the problem. It is merely a symptom. The size of government is a directly inverse reflection of the responsibility and initiative of the people. We should be most grieved by the absence of self-government in "we, the people."

Recall for a moment my allusion in chapter 6 to 1 Samuel 8 as the birthplace of statism. What is striking in that ancient text is how consistent things have remained throughout history. For millennia, the pattern remains the same: when people abdicate their responsibilities, a larger civil magistrate steps in. In the United States, the "hockey stick" growth in the size of government has directly coincided with the most socially destructive period in American history (see chapter 3). In his masterful work *The Fractured Republic*, Yuval Levin reveals that the growth of federal bureaucracy further coincided with the decline of our great "mediating institutions"—family, church, local community organizations, trade clubs, and so on.

The decline of these mediating institutions has left society "hollowed out in the middle spaces where a free society forms."[46] A society without strong mediating institutions engages in a tug-of-war between individualism and heavy centralized collectivism. The problem is that our society is used to the benefits of mediating institutions that have cared for the "general welfare" from our inception. Because we have turned our backs on the politics of subsidiarity, localism, and a commitment to community and covenant, the state has filled the gap that individualism could never fill. We did not hire the government to fill the post; we abandoned the post—and left government no choice but to step in.

None of this is to say government *can* or *should* fill this void, only that *it will always attempt to do so when self-government fails.* Warnings about this reality came from the very founders whose political philosophy we hold dear. Indeed, from Madison to Adams to Hamilton to Franklin, even a cursory review of their exhortations hits us right between the eyes. The American doctrine of limited government was intended only for a responsible citizenry, rooted in character, morality, and self-government.

The self-attesting evidence is found in every controversial discussion about budget cuts or program reductions. Can anyone point to a consensus willingness *on a societal level* to eliminate some part of government we dislike? How well has it worked in this modern era to roll back an entitlement? What wrath and fury do congressional representatives face from constituents when they propose some form of reduction, cut, or sacrifice? In this case, we are not talking about the corruption of special interests, but about the tyranny of the majority. It wants all the sugars and sweets that big government offers, but reserves the right to complain when it gets the bill.

We have a representative form of government in the United States. We elect the leaders who pass laws and spend money. They are spending the money that the people have asked them to spend—or they would not be spending it. Does that fact absolve our representatives of their moral and political responsibility? Of course not! Despite the bipolar nature of their constituents' requests, our representatives swear a duty to the Constitution.

No doubt, we deserve better leadership than we have received. But my point is more foundational and must not be missed: in our form of government, our leaders not only *represent* the people, they *reflect* the people. Alexander Fraser Tytler warned that our democracy would be threatened when the people discover they can "vote themselves generous gifts from the public treasury." The evidence of this truism could not be more abundant in modern civic life.

How Far We've Fallen

Don't misunderstand me. Government should not get a pass for bad governance. Government is riddled with corruption, incompetence, dishonesty, and failure. It is no surprise to see American citizens dissatisfied with their elected representatives. The one thing in my adult life that I have seen government do well is cater to the crony needs of powerful interests (see chapter 6). Americans often don't know if they should be more aghast at the incompetence or the corruption in the system.

Crony capitalism is one of the major reasons for our national obsession with federal politics, and national apathy with local politics. The opportunity for real, bottom-up transformation in our political system is far more infectious at the local level, yet only a big, bureaucratic, all-encompassing federal government can scratch our national political itches. We have a big, centralized federal government because the people want one and have put their entire political enthusiasm into the federal space.

Local politics has become of interest only to real estate developers or those with a stake in a zoning or regulatory approval. The cronyism embedded in the local politic—the view that city and county politics essentially exist to dole out favors to a connected class of lobbyists and special interests—has an insidious double effect: (1) it feeds on itself with even greater corruption and unopposed cronyism at the local level, and (2) it empowers a view of the federal government that is more messianic than limited. Not only would a corrected view of local politics—rooted in good governance, property rights, and civic life—purify the city, county, and state levels of the cronyism, it would also shift the weights presently loaded on the federal scales in the direction of local responsibility.

Ronald Reagan famously said that among the most dangerous words in the English language were these: "I'm from the government and I'm here to help." Conservatism and the Reagan revolution were rooted, at least intellectually, in a desire to renew self-determination and self-government. Those who share my view of government's limited role were distraught to hear President Obama's vision of an American civic life resembling the European democratic social model. Promises to pay off student debt, to alter corporate pay, to give everyone free health care—in short, to place the federal government at the center of American life—rightly frighten those who value the founders' beliefs about the right relationship between citizen and state.

Why Blame Washington?

So why are we blaming Washington, DC, for all of our problems now? If we do not believe they are capable of being the cure for all our problems, how can we believe they are the source of all our problems? As our crisis of responsibility has increased, the American conversation is becoming less partisan, more cultural, and increasingly rhyming with "what is government going to do to fix my problem?" Some politicians still talk about the righteous effects of deregulation and increased freedom, but does anyone believe a message of less government to address the social ills of our day is politically viable?

We applaud politicians promising to save our jobs, bring money to our districts, and lower our monthly expenses (even the non-tax expenses over which they have no control). We ask our politicians to promote higher home prices, but blast them for housing crises. We ask them to lower our health insurance premium costs, but blast them for their intervening in the health markets. We do not pause to recognize how obnoxious all their campaign bluster really is or how absurd their stump speech promises really are.

More importantly, we do not seem to consider that, in many ways, we have adopted the Left's view of government. Our first instinct is often not to consider the individual, whose natural rights form the basis of our society. Instead, when faced with any external aggravation we wonder how a politician can fix it. This mindset has become embedded into our social consciousness as we have abandoned so much of what has made the American experiment so remarkable.

Right-sizing the federal government is not going to happen quickly. The best we can hope for is incremental or gradual progress. But even gradual improvement cannot begin until we, the people, accept greater responsibility for the outcomes in our own lives. In this crisis of responsibility, we have every right to hold elected officials accountable for what they do. We should move heaven and earth to avoid "bartering our freedom"—and yet that is the inevitable result whenever we fail to govern ourselves.

If we are to resolve this crisis, we must see a broad acceptance of this basic truth: *with great freedom comes great responsibility.* When we rediscover responsibility, we'll create a virtuous cycle that produces more freedom. And it begins with you and me.

11

THE RESPONSIBILITY REMEDY
Ten Ways You Can Compete, Prepare, Defend, and Get Ahead

Success on any major scale requires you to accept responsibility. In the final analysis, the one quality that all successful people have is the ability to take on responsibility.

—MICHAEL KORDA

Action springs not from thought, but from a readiness for responsibility.

—DIETRICH BONHOEFFER

My aspirations for this book and, indeed, this chapter are quite humble. I did not set out to write a comprehensive policy manual on a topic as broad and far-reaching as *responsibility*. My highest hope is this book provokes a change in thinking and helps shift how we see what we want to change in our society. Many of the diverse and complex issues I have tackled do not allow for a simple or succinct solution. In addition, our crisis of responsibility has been building for at least a full generation and cannot be resolved simply by writing a book or preaching a sermon. Nevertheless, some practical suggestions would be helpful as to how you and me, the people on Main Street, can cure our addiction to blame before I pull it all together with a broader cultural takeaway in chapter 12.

I am an incrementalist. I believe problems created incrementally are most often solved incrementally, as well. This tactical approach to life has theological foundations:

> He told them another parable: "The kingdom of heaven is like a mustard seed, which a man took and planted in his field.[32] Though it is the smallest of all seeds, yet when it grows, it is the largest of garden plants and becomes a tree, so that the birds come and perch in its branches.[33]
>
> He told them still another parable: "The kingdom of heaven is like yeast that a woman took and mixed into about sixty pounds of flour until it worked all through the dough." (Matthew 13:31–33)

Seeds take time to grow; yeast takes time to work. I have every hope we will remedy the plight of those feeling disenfranchised in the global economy immediately. However, history teaches us that deep and meaningful cultural changes often take years, even decades to take hold. Our culture did not inherit a crisis of responsibility overnight, but over a generational period of time beginning in the mid-1960s. It has marinated ever since in the seasonings of humanism, secular liberalism, and moral relativism. What we see in culture today is a reasonably consistent extension of the seeds planted then. The burden now is to evaluate what broad cultural endeavors are needed to resolve the responsibility crisis (chapter 12) and, in this chapter, identify what individual measures, steps, actions, and behaviors you can take to improve our cultural lot and advance the cause of human flourishing. In other words, *what can you do?*

The list of ten practical things you can do is intended to be bottom-up in nature, whereas the focus of the next chapter is more top-down in orientation. Many experts debate whether cultural transformation is catalyzed by top-down or bottom-up forces. Years ago, University of Virginia sociologist Dr. James Davison Hunter deeply affected my thinking on the subject. He suggested that top-down forces nearly always set off history's major transformations. They did so not only via significant impact through large institutions, but also by leveraging the networks formed amongst various elites.

As we'll see in the next chapter, Dr. Hunter is profoundly correct. The move to create culture-forming and culture-transforming networks to affect our society's top-down institutions is paramount. And yet, there simply can be no denial that big things can and do happen as a result of the faithful and seemingly miniscule endeavors of a few. In addition, we are concerned about society at-large because we are concerned about people—individuals, families, and communities. While we seek societal transformation, we should pursue tools for the flourishing of individuals.

So, should we focus on top-down or bottom-up solutions? The answer is an emphatic *yes*—to both.

Ten Things You Can Do

The list that follows is not meant to be a financial planning checklist, though it makes sense to include a financial focus given my background as a wealth management professional. The focus is not merely on saving habits or investment returns, but also includes a variety of arenas in which one's thinking and commitments can either create heartache or substantially improve your ability to navigate through the present cultural challenges. The list is in no way intended to be comprehensive or convey a particular order of priority. Rather, it highlights the lowest-hanging fruit, areas where action would surely move the needle in your life. Faithfully implementing best practices delivers two additional benefits: (1) an example to others, and (2) the fruit that faithful wisdom itself generates. Neither of these advantages should be discounted.

To help resolve our cultural crisis of responsibility and pursue a life of freedom and virtue, I suggest the following:

1. Thoroughly repudiate defeatism and victimhood in your own life—*even when you've actually been victimized.*

The second part of this admonition presents the greatest challenge, for most of us have been wronged at some point in life. But if we do not overcome our slights, they will overcome us. When our way of mindset centers on all the ways we have been wronged, the temptation to abdicate responsibility, even subconsciously, is simply too strong. The "just toughen up" crowd might appreciate this counsel, but would couch it as a call to grit your teeth and power through the injustices you've suffered. But there remains a better way. Repudiate defeatism *because* you crave an abundant life of joy, and repudiate defeatism *by* craving an abundant life of joy. Make that abundant life of joy both the means and the end.

This approach requires a specific anthropological understanding, the awareness that you are created in the image of God with inherent dignity. This awareness of basic spiritual and transcendent truths doesn't speak merely to your relationship with God and what He expects of you (though it does that, too). Victimhood strips you of dignity and gives control and power to external forces, whether personal or impersonal. This surrender of control impedes the life of joy and strips you of the freedom you were made to enjoy.

Your view of yourself cannot be one of "me against the world." Believing that your boss, spouse, customers, or political leaders are all out to get you results in a life shaped by fear, not love—and certainly not joy. Might a spouse, boss, neighbor, or politician actually have it in for you? It's possible, I suppose. Yet even then, the productive response is not despair or defeatism, but courageous faithfulness. I've never seen someone who lives in a perpetual state of victimhood make good decisions. I've never seen defeatism result in anything but being defeated, or victimization create anything but a victim.

A life of resilience will inevitably be a life of joy. As any joyful person knows, such resilience is fundamentally a matter of outlook and perspective. The decision to reject any suggestion that you are a victim of external circumstances is the sine qua non for those pursuing success in our complex modern life.

2. Completely rethink your perspective on higher education, for yourself or your children.

Critics might suggest a straw man interpretation of my point by saying I'm rejecting the merits of a college education, but that is patently false. What I'm suggesting is we acknowledge helpful truths.

- ▶ Is college a prerequisite for everyone? Of course not.
- ▶ Does college guarantee one an economically comfortable life? Of course not.
- ▶ Absent a college degree, will one be doomed to financial failure? Of course not.
- ▶ Is all student debt a good idea, regardless of the school, the subject matter, and the person's unique goals? Of course not.

If we could fully grasp two truths, the scam that higher education has become would die: (1) *a college degree doesn't guarantee success*, and (2) *not having a college degree doesn't guarantee failure.*

Inverting those two statements is what has fed the current college monster.

So what are you to think? Am I suggesting college is a waste of time, a net negative for our society? Quite the contrary. As I detailed in chapter 9, I am highly critical of the business model and what is taught in today's system, but I passionately believe in the inherent value of a higher education, particularly in certain fields of study college ought to facilitate. I see incredible value to the college years of one's life being used to further solidify goals, interests, and passions. College ought to represent a unique opportunity to exercise responsibility, meet deadlines, and be intellectually and spiritually challenged.

I'm not encouraging a universal rejection of college, but a realistic cost-benefits analysis of it, as opposed to making vanilla assumptions. "One size fits all" is generally a bad idea in any part of life, but when it costs $250,000, it can be financially fatal. The diversity of gifts, aspirations, goals, and circumstances invites a plethora of educational possibilities—trade school, apprenticeship, blue-collar work, entrepreneurial endeavors, and—yes—college. I suspect that, even after a thorough analysis, most parents will still want their children to achieve a four-year undergraduate degree. I am simply suggesting you ingrain the two fundamental truths above before starting that journey.

If you or your children do not go to college expecting a guaranteed outcome, you or they will be less likely to stumble into a crisis of responsibility when it doesn't deliver that outcome. The young adult years are pivotal parts of life. Parents and students alike should enter those years armed against disillusionment.

3. Prepare your children for economic self-reliance.

There was a time in my career in wealth management where the most intense financial generational burden was the daunting task of caring for one's parents in their senior years. In fifteen years, that has completely changed. Now for every conversation we have about planning senior care, we have ten conversations about parents needing to financially support their adult children.

This phenomenon has been blamed on the challenges of the post-2008 economy to some degree—and for good reason. But, as Senator Ben Sasse has suggested in his masterful book *The Vanishing American Adult: Our Coming-of-Age Crisis—and How to Rebuild a Culture of Self-Reliance*, much of the problem does not require scolding the millennial generation, but rather a shift in how we prepare them for adult life. Perpetual adolescence is a systemic problem and, though it is primarily a cultural one, carries grave economic implications, as well.

The danger of including it in this book meant for a broad audience is that it doesn't allow for the inevitable particulars of each and every family. But my underlying point is this: instilling a culture of self-reliance in your kids is not only good and loving parenting, it is also vitally important for economic well-being—both for you and for society. Household formation has been decimated by the "extended odyssey phase."[47] Financial pro formas, parents' own aspirations, our children's dignity, and the well-being of society doesn't allow for the years between twenty-one and thirty-five to be merely a time of nonproductive discovery.

As Sasse rightly says, guard against this peril by preparing your kids to be "fully formed, vivacious, appealing, resilient, self-reliant, problem-solving souls who see themselves as called to love and serve their neighbors."[48]

4. Consider reengaging the lost world of local politics.

Most damage is done at the local level of politics. I confess to this being a case of the pot calling the kettle black, having been a federal politics junkie for my entire adult life and most of my childhood, as well. I wish I could say that by engaging local politics you will become less cynical and frustrated, but I must warn you—it's highly likely to get worse. I dealt with crony capitalism more in chapter 6 and argued that crony interests prevent a host of well-meaning people from getting involved in local politics in chapter 10. Nevertheless, the need is overwhelming in our cities, counties, and states.

We need greater competence and greater integrity. The dilemma we face is this: the most competent and honest in society have found the world of local politics repugnant (for good reason, most of the time). In their absence, ne'er-do-wells or worse eagerly fill the vacuum. But who fills the halls of Congress eventually? Former state senate and state assembly members. Who gets elected to these state positions? Former members of county boards and city councils. Local politics is generally a training ground for state and federal politics. Thus, our apathy for local politics leaves us with terrible consequences now for our cities and terrible future consequences for everywhere else.

Truth be told, plenty of fantastic people enter local civic leadership for no other reason than to serve their communities. By no means do I want to paint with a broad brush, but we have a systemic problem. There are not enough high-quality candidates in the local domain and not enough citizens engaged on the topics and issues that matter most. For example, city councils and county boards have done more damage to property rights than any liberal Supreme Court could have done in a lifetime. City councils and county boards control zoning laws, which have proven to be extraordinary tools for central planning and statism.

The business-friendliness of a community is often either established or destroyed at the local level, because the general process by which business gets done is determined by the tax, regulatory, and enforcement framework. When I say cronyism festers at the local level, it's because local officials are most guilty of making special handouts of public dollars (or selectively waiving tax liabilities, the reciprocal expression of the exact same thing).

So much of the American quality of life is a by-product of our local community leadership. Protecting and enhancing that quality of life requires men and women of responsibility to lead with diligence, character, and competence. And for those who, like me, believe in subsidiarity, the best defense against a far-removed federal government intruding into a local community—whether about homelessness, school choice, park safety, police training, or water resources—is not to give them a reason to do so. Strong local governance always and forever limits the need for a stronger, more oppressive federal government.

5. Flee the cult of home ownership and home price appreciation in your thinking and behavior about real estate.

I am not telling you to abandon the goal or practice of home ownership, nor am I encouraging a drop in the market value of anyone's home. The indisputable fact is that our societal addiction to home ownership helped create a financial crisis—and postcrisis attitudes don't indicate evidence of a lesson learned. One can achieve a great financial feat in buying a home, and an even greater financial feat in paying for it. My criticism here is more focused on two concerns:

1. the individual obsession with short-term home prices that treats a house more like a trading card than a home
2. a bipartisan policy response that assumes pushing housing prices up is a desired end in and of itself

Regarding the first, specific and significant actions that created the inflated housing prices are not taking place now—lack of income qualification, negative amortizing loans, and the disregard for down payment. However, the *mentality that created and fueled them is still alive and well*—the belief that a home is more of an economic tool than a community-building place to live in and raise a family. That short-term thinking about the home itself breeds reckless financial decisions—stretching to afford too much, maintaining inadequate protective equity, and misunderstanding the very basics of economic home ownership.

As to the second, it is utterly perverse for policymakers to believe it is their job to promote rising home values. It's also highly discriminatory—are there not two sides to every home purchase? Since when is it appropriate for a politician to root for one side over the other in a private transaction? Will home prices organically rise in a free market economy as wages rise, quality of life increases, and modest inflationary forces surface? Very likely so. But that organic increase of real estate values is subject to extensive external influences (interest rates, supply, demand, new construction, labor market conditions, etc.) and needs no input from cheerleading politicians. Besides, policies promoting higher house prices discriminate for sellers against buyers and likely favor older, wealthier people over younger people of lesser means. *This discriminatory policy trend should be creating populist rage.*

Why do politicians and individuals still tout the supposed advantages of higher home prices? One simple reason is most people's personal balance sheets have so little liquidity that they want the mirage of real estate appreciation for the psychological wealth effect. Certainly those about to sell a home have a justifiable reason to desire a higher price. But what our society needs right now is to value household formation and *the process of home ownership, not merely the end itself.*

The discipline of saving for a down payment on a home is a virtue-creating act. Protecting one's credit to be able to ably and responsibly borrow to buy a home is a virtue-creating act. Succeeding in a job to be in a position to buy—and then keep—a home is a virtue-creating act. When you've sacrificed to acquire a home, you appreciate it, you cultivate it, you value it, and you become responsible members of the local community. All of this is what Jay Richards has called the "virtuous circle" of home ownership—"wise behavior makes it possible to acquire a home, and then the acquisition of the home reinforces wise behavior."[49]

Some people should not buy a home. It's silly for people to deplete their retirement accounts and liquid savings to buy a home based on attractive interest rates—with no way to afford maintenance, insurance, or taxes. Renting is not a sociological pariah; it is very often a wise and prudent, if not downright attractive, thing to do. How much labor market immobility—the sad state of labor dynamism we discussed in chapter 5—is a by-product of people being handcuffed to a home they never should have purchased?

The truth is that the biggest financial mistake most on Main Street will ever make will be the result of flawed thinking about home ownership. For many, the wisest thing they will ever do will be to exercise prudence, patience, thrift, and virtue in home-buying decisions.

6. Reject the social safety net when you can and choose the more challenging but fulfilling path of self-reliance.

I know this point will generate the most opposition, and I understand why. There is an apparently galling lack of empathy in a financially comfortable business owner like myself telling others to reject society's cushions. I get that. But my exhortation here is rooted in empathy, not indifference. Yes, I am financially comfortable and live in an affluent community, but I have not always been such. I've tried to avoid personal biography as much as possible in this book to protect against any accusations of self-congratulatory ego. But this is a subject as near and dear to my heart as any in the book. I believe passionately, sincerely, and empathetically that able-bodied people abusing the societal safety net is not only wrong but economically counterproductive and existentially fatal. It is economically counterproductive because of the irresistible allure of dependency. It is existentially fatal because it denies the dignity of achievement through perseverance.

I want a robust system of job creation that promotes human flourishing for all, but I am sympathetic to the realities of desperate situations. I support a culture of assistance in the context of subsidiarity. I'm not blind to some of the darkest and scariest experiences many suffer. My advice here deals not with those situations, but with the ones in the middle where a real choice exists—to choose the hard but better path and reject social benefits, or to choose the easy but self-defeating option and accept them.

What I'm referencing here is the "stretch" or "abuse" of the safety net—the use of a doctor's note to collect disability when it's not really required, for example, or the manipulation of unemployment benefits outside their intended scope. Instead of this self-corrupting behavior, I am encouraging you to take a path that produces the virtue of achievement, the satisfaction of earned success, and the empowerment that comes only from overcoming adversity.

7. Find your joy in production, not consumption.

Consumption isn't wrong. But my advice aims to reinforce a time-tested totem pole for that which creates real meaning and contentment in life. First, review some important basic economic truisms. When human beings creatively transform matter into resources, they create wealth. In this sense, there can be no wealth creation without production. And in a more fundamentally obvious sense, one's ability to consume must come after his or her ability to produce—you can't afford to consume until you first produce something of value. Consumption for the sake of consumption destroys value. Output and value creation can only come from production. Increasing consumption is always the *result* of growth, not the cause of it.

Therefore, discovering valuable ways to serve and produce for others is what causes economic growth. Confusion about this basic truth has led to all sorts of economic malady. But the confusion has created even worse existential problems. We live in a consumer-driven society, where short-term highs can be achieved with the latest app or video game. But decades of study about "earned success" reinforce the fact that the act of production brings sustainable value and substantive internal satisfaction. It fulfills higher needs in our hierarchy of longings.

Understanding these priorities, and consciously construct-ing your life around them, engenders gratitude, facilitates a life of useful service to others, and creates intrinsic value when you inherit all the rewards of meaningful productivity and purpose.

8. View *and treat* family as the economic building block of society.

With this advice, I am suggesting more than the intellectual awareness that the fragmenting family deteriorates the social safety net, creates inefficient allocation of resources, and undermines societal development. Understanding the inverse relationship between strong families and poverty is important, but it's not at the heart of my advice here. Also necessary, but not sufficient, is an awareness that family formation builds wealth and family dissolution destroys wealth. What we need in this day and age is not merely the correct answers on a social science quiz, but correct living, modeling the value of strong family units in our own lives.

The macro contribution of healthy families in our society comes from the micro combination of healthy families. The macro math does not exist outside of the micro; it results from it! In this case, we are talking about the greatest economic cycle of virtue ever known to mankind. Married people have embedded incentive to produce, because they care for the other member of the marriage. Therefore, resources are shared and not wasted. Children then become the greatest incentive the world has ever seen for married couples to produce, preserve, and grow.

Marriage civilizes, organizes, and motivates people. It facilitates organization, division of labor, efficiency, routine, and structure in a fundamental way. In living out the positive social implications of this reality, loving parents model it to their children, who then grow up more likely to replicate the same productive dynamic in their own family structures. Conversely, single parenthood and divorce produce statistically worse economic implications for women and an overwhelming increase in social welfare programs. Cohesive families create structure not only for the intellectual and moral development of children, but for their economic provision, as well.

I find it hard to believe anyone reading this book doesn't already know all of this to be true about family at the macro level. So why include it? Because I am advocating for us to practice it *at the micro level.*

I'm asking that we rethink the faddish celebration of late and deferred marriages. I am suggesting that the economic struggles experienced by people ages twenty-five to thirty-four in the modern economy are directly correlated to marriages being at an all-time low for that age demographic. I am encouraging resilience, problem solving, commitment, and communication in our marriages, versus the easy pull of the divorce lever. I am distinguishing marriage from cohabitation, both morally and economically. I am celebrating children, not viewing them as a nuisance or inconvenience. I am suggesting to young men that that they can dramatically enhance their eligibility for marriage by developing productive work skills and capabilities that bring value to society. I am encouraging a greater emphasis on hard work and a lower priority on video game entertainment. (I would actually prefer the elimination of video games, but I digress.)

The deterioration of family creates an overwhelming negative feedback loop and a tension that hampers our economic productivity. This book is not a marriage manual or child-rearing handbook, but when we place a high value on family, the positive feedback loop we create is a potent force, not only for society, but in each of our own lives.

9. Administer your own personal finances proactively, defensively, opportunistically, and prudently.

The era of middle-class families doing no budgeting or financial planning, pursuing no contingency arrangements, avoiding risk management, and having no plan for savings and investment—yet coveting the results of those who have—needs to end. When you have an adequate reserve account, the negative forces of job displacement can be managed very differently. You think about mobility and career options differently when you have been funding a retirement investment account for years. To determine financial objectives and organize disciplined steps to meet those objectives is both simple and far too rare.

For those who object, I can preemptively write the rebuttal, because it is as predictable as it is unconvincing. No, financial planning and preparation are not unique luxuries for people who already have abundant economic resources. The stakes may be higher when there is more money in your net worth statement, but every adult can organize a basic financial structure. For many people, it will involve diverse and even sophisticated investment planning. For others, it may mean debating whether you can afford contributing $100 or $200 each month to their employer's 401(k) plan. Whatever it means in your situation, you can exponentially enhance your ability to defend against unexpected economic woes by engaging the basic process of financial seriousness.

A perception exists that wealthy, corporate executives can do financial planning, but the blue-collar family struggling to get ahead cannot. Not only is this nothing but pitiful avoidance behavior, it also becomes a self-fulfilling prophecy. It ignores a surprising reality in human nature that professional wealth managers like myself know all too well: *a lot of people on the upper rungs of the economic ladder don't do a bang-up job of financial planning either!* A plethora of high earners find themselves underfunded, over-indebted, and underprepared for life's unexpected. They fall back on the same excuses as those with less wealth to work with.

Overcoming our crisis of responsibility is the subject of this book, and financial planning requires responsibility. Pursuing a basic checklist of financial preparation is a paradigm-shifting way to prepare for whatever happens next in this new global economy.

10. Be a generous, charitable giver.

When you give generously to charity, not only do you meet the needs of others, but you also receive back multiples of what you give. It's a long-understood and glorious mystery for those who practice philanthropy. In this way, sacrificial giving can be one of the most selfish things you do, because it often does as much or more for you as it does the recipients of your gift. I wouldn't wish to defend this claim intellectually, but it is a paradoxical truth. The more you give, the more you get.

There is also the underlying fact that a virtuous society picking up the load for the welfare state requires generous, charitable giving. But beyond that reality, I suggest that your commitment to supporting the churches, schools, charities, and humanitarian organizations you believe in produces an unquantifiable satisfaction and reward. I do not mean mere appeasement of guilt, nor am I describing anything like karma. I am addressing a reality of human nature—when we faithfully and sacrificially give, the act itself fills a priceless reservoir of joy.

A responsible society is a charitable society. And a charitable society begins with each person giving according to his or her means.

Is there more you can do personally to help resolve our crisis of responsibility? Of course. Overcoming the cultural crisis will also require a cultural response (the subject of the next and final chapter), but responsibility begins in our homes. My intent with this list is to get you thinking about what you can do to better insulate your own family against the challenges we face. The stakes are so high—and the need so heavy—that we truly do need all hands on deck.

Main Street has asked the elites in this populist uprising of late to quit acting like they have all the answers. By enacting the ten items I have listed in this chapter, Main Street will go a long way toward telling the elites, "We don't need you after all. We've got this."

12
THE CULTURAL REMEDY FOR MAIN STREET
A Vision for a Free and Virtuous Society

We do not need more material development, we need more
spiritual development. We do not need more intellectual power,
we need more moral power. We do not need more knowledge, we
need more character. We do not need more government, we need
more culture. We do not need more law, we need more religion. We
do not need more of the things that are seen, we need more of the
things that are unseen. It is on that side of life that it is desirable to
put the emphasis at the present time. If that side be strengthened,
the other side will take care of itself.

–PRESIDENT CALVIN COOLIDGE

Thomas Sowell's masterful book *Intellectuals and Society* (2009) explored the topic of public intelligentsia. Sowell asked what fruits society has reaped from the intellectual class and how we became so obsessed with what this class says, especially when the demand for their opinions was almost entirely self-manufactured. As Sowell put it, "The role that they aspire to play in society at large can only be achieved by them to the extent that the rest of society accepts what they say uncritically and fails to examine their track record."

Sowell condemned a charlatan class of journalists, academics, and politicians who uncritically accepted the elite's anointed vision for the world. The solution, says Sowell, is to not exempt public intellectuals from external validation tests. An arrogance in modern collectivism has led to the Left advocating for "surrogate decision making." Because the elite's vision of the anointed was transferred from intellectuals to outfits like the *New York Times* and various public teacher unions, those who would strip elites of their decision-making authority in society now face a much harder task. (In other words, the leftist and elitist vision for society as permeated into the mainstream.)[50]

What Sowell could not have anticipated in 2009 was that by 2016—only seven years later—a global movement would arise to say *enough* to the elites and intellectuals responsible for so much flawed ideology and policy in public life. The charlatan class of journalists, academics, and politicians is as alive as ever, but it must now contend with a vigorous and even angry public resistance, dissatisfied with an increasing level of incompetence, unproductivity, and unfulfilled promises coming from the silos of the self-anointed.

In the aftermath of the great recession, governmental gridlock, and secular below-trend economic growth, the tide of public sentiment has turned. Around the world—from Detroit to London, Chicago to Brussels, Middletown, Ohio, to Tokyo, Japan—skepticism, if not downright revolt, has metastasized. We have lost faith in the ability of society's architects to provide for the public good, deliver on utopian promises, promote a safe society, and dispatch economic prosperity.

For those like Sowell (and this author) who bemoan the influence of this allegedly enlightened class, this paradigm shift carries the potential of promise. There is great hope to be had in a public that rejects unproven or failed ideas. The cultural flow that allowed the elites to be unchallenged when delivering their harmful yet highly consequential worldview has begun to reverse. Thus, the present cultural dissatisfaction has the potential of being a constructive building block for a better tomorrow.

If our society is to resist the arrogance, and even tyranny, of this "establishment" class, we must face our own crisis of responsibility head-on. The people appear ready to reject a top-down societal structure; but meanwhile, our preparation for assuming the bottom-up responsibilities of self-governance is wholly inadequate. We lack the social and cultural framework needed for the transfer of power from disinterested third-party elites to societal stakeholders with skin in the game. The seeds of discontent have been sown—rightly so. But assuming the mantle of moral leadership requires a moral readiness, an underlying sense of responsibility that is the nonnegotiable prerequisite for a free and virtuous society.

At the heart of our responsibility crisis is an increasingly heated love affair with victimhood—we are addicted to blame. And all of us have lusted after it one way or another—conservatives and liberals, on the outside and the inside, rural America and cosmopolitan America. We have all found different bogeymen to blame for the things that dissatisfy us, but they are bogeymen nonetheless. The Left caricaturizes financial fat cats and corporate executives while the Right demonizes journalists and politicos. Kernels of truth turn to wholesale excuses for passivity, inactivity, and apathy. All too often, our society has fixated on what has been done to us, whether real or imagined, while losing a healthy and rugged fixation on self-reliance and actualization.

We err when we delineate responsibility from morality. A sustainable culture of accountability requires a basic foundation of ethics. It inevitably demands social standards, norms, and values. Our present culture isn't merely lazy; we are reaping what has been sown by moral relativism and ethical agnosticism. The vicious cycle caused by our cultural crisis of responsibility is a by-product of the deterioration of our cultural character.

Hope Beyond the Blame

All is not lost. Our rich cultural inheritance is formed from the greatest parts of the human spirit and divine providence. Re-moralization is possible. Individual responsibility deteriorated in one generation. Surely, it can be restored in one, as well. But it will not happen until we end the blame game.

What I have attempted to do in this book is to correct the false narrative that every impediment to prosperity is caused by some unfair, undefined, uncontrollable external force.

Globalization has created entirely new challenges, but it doesn't excuse an inadequately dynamic labor force. The financial crisis revealed a horrific meatloaf of bad policy and bad actors, but it does not excuse an individual for refusing to keep personal financial commitments. Government policies and regulations have wreaked havoc on economic incentives, but they do not excuse a pitiful work ethic. China can manufacture products cheaper than many domestic companies and Mexico has added labor at the lower end of the wage scale. However, those facts do not excuse someone who refuses to develop new job skills or adjust to economic realities that offer both challenges and opportunities. Wall Street has often behaved recklessly, but that behavior does not justify a reckless Main Street. Automation and digital innovation create a daunting headwind for parts of the labor force, but that does not unlearn over one hundred years of lessons about "creative destruction" and innovation. Higher education has failed millions, but that does not mean it can disengage from society. Government has grown far too big, but that does not mean the people should capitulate and become entirely dependent on the state.

In each case, I have tried to demonstrate the prima facie validity of the alleged bogeyman, to acknowledge the real challenge at least, and any full-blown misbehavior at worst. And yet, with every threat to opportunity for every class of Americans, we consistently see a path forward to true prosperity and fulfillment—if we refuse to play the blame game and reassert responsibility.

No one should think that I am offering policymakers and elites a pass by consciously and emphatically focusing on responsibility. Yet I suspect some will do so, if for no other reason than to dodge responsibility themselves. It is a dilemma as old as Adam in the garden—when your own culpability is exposed, simply cry, "What about other guy [or gal]?!" My pleas for overcoming a crisis of responsibility on Main Street should not be read as a vindication of institutions and elites.

The crisis of responsibility is personal, it is individual, and it is bottom-up. And yet, it is *also* institutional, corporate, and top-down. The two are not binary or mutually exclusive. We need responsible decision making and leadership from the pillars of society. I have attempted to drive home the need for leadership on a number of issues:

- ▶ To stop using housing policy to drive social aims
- ▶ To create a financial underwriting policy that promotes "skin in the game"
- ▶ To craft policies that drive labor market dynamism and invest resources into retraining, education, and reinvention
- ▶ To add tax deductibility for skill development outside of one's present job field
- ▶ To completely overhaul the relationship between the state and crony corporate actors, whose corrupt

peddling of influence has shredded faith in American business and commerce
- ▶ To develop a system of school choice, utilizing both charter schools and tax credits, to empower parents and students to achieve their educational aims
- ▶ To reinitiate assimilation as the driving force behind our immigration policy, so that American culture and patriotic pride are valued
- ▶ To terminate the present business model of higher education and excessive student debt, and rethink a system of disengaged university chancellors, bureaucrats, and professors
- ▶ To right-size government programs and budgets to promote fiscal sanity, solvency, and the dignity of the American people

From legislators to bankers, corporate leaders to lobbyists, educators to policymakers, this book has offered no immunity to anyone. Nor have I merely lobbed complaints at the leadership class. I have offered a constructive set of policy reformulations. The challenge in a book very consciously designed to be an overview is that a detailed blueprint for all social maladies is simply not possible. I am neither arrogant nor naïve enough to suggest that the prescriptions I have proposed are comprehensive cures. But I do suggest that in the major categories of school choice, crony capitalism, labor market dynamism, and student debt reform, we have in these pages a highly effective launching pad for truly respecting and addressing the policy sources of populist rage without ignoring the elephant in the room.

The burden of living a fulfilling life belongs on the individual. To do so effectively, we must eliminate impediments to individual responsibility. Crony capitalism and a discriminatory educational system enables actors to avoid responsibility and often facilitates their victimhood. A member of society who refuses to learn a new marketable job skill is a victim of his own laziness; but a member of society also becomes a victim when denied access to the doors of education or enterprise made available to other select groups. He or she ought not to embrace a victim mentality, but they should be viewed differently than those who create their own estranged circumstances. That is why our approach must be a both/and—dealing with shortcomings in policy and also addressing the overwhelming need for greater initiative, self-reliance, and responsibility.

We do too much to feed angst without curing it. We can caricature successful corporate executives as "fat cats," but that does nothing to heal the covetousness driving the caricaturing. We love the idea of "recalling" politicians who disappoint us, but that does nothing to restore responsibility to the voters who elected them to begin with. The need of the hour is to empower a renewed sense of responsibility, including facing the consequences of our actions. Our crisis of responsibility cannot be overcome if we are insulated by a perpetual safety net from the consequences of our actions. We reap what we sow, and so it should be.

The Way Home

I suppose it is true that my adult life consists of being on "the inside" of all the best offered by the global economy and information age. I work in the cosmopolitan field of investment finance and maintain offices in the affluent communities of Newport Beach, California, and New York City. I am married and have three children who attend private school. I live in a context of comfort and convenience, despite not growing up in anything of the sort. I could never write *Hillbilly Elegy* because my life has not been that life. But like J. D. Vance, I have an insatiable compassion and empathy for people who are not presently tasting a life of opportunity and prosperity. Not a bone in my body indicts anyone in this crisis of responsibility because of a cosmopolitan or moral superiority complex.

My every waking passion desires that all of God's creation find "the good life." I believe in the aspirational society, and, more importantly, I believe in the extraordinary peace and contentment produced by earned success. Success is not limited to the educated, elite, or some "higher rung" of society. The free and virtuous society I long to see—the America I believe in—is exceptional because all may pursue their unalienable rights to life, liberty, and happiness with a shared creed of faith, values, and character.

If I believed an opportunity society could flourish merely by demonizing the institutional forces and elites that have become persona non grata in our society, I would wholeheartedly join the chorus. And to the extent that constructive policy criticism is needed, it is my responsibility as a stakeholder in society to join the song. But because I genuinely love those most disenfranchised and disaffected in our society, I cannot pretend that all the pain is someone else's fault. A culture of responsibility and scapegoatism cannot peacefully coexist. America is an ownership society, not only in our brand of economics, but in the very spirit with which we tackle adversity. Restoring our culture will not be easy, but no elitist or globalist enemy of any sort will ever be vanquished until we do.

Individualism has always been a hallmark of American life, but it has fallen out of favor now. We need thriving cultural institutions now more than ever in the face of cultural shifts and economic realities, but they have been suffocated by ineffectual, top-down governance. It is not my contention that we must choose between the two and shift from enlightened collectivism to rugged individualism to find our savior. We do need to restore individual responsibility, but individualism becomes merely a buzzword when not partnered with mediating institutions.

Replacing top-down statism and elitism will happen only when we restore strong families, communities, churches, schools, and civic organizations. Subsidiarity must be restored, not only as a political or philanthropic philosophy, but also *as a vision for public life.* That means individuals engaged in those arenas have a responsibility to value the work they do and the greater role they play in benefitting society at large. Fraternal organizations must become more than LinkedIn entries. They should become part of the fabric of how our communities live, how we serve one another, and how we think about public life. We are engaged in solving a "chicken or the egg" cultural problem, a cycle of irresponsibility that will take great resolve to overcome.

As I have grown up, my understanding of organized society has changed—*a lot.* I no longer believe in the simplistic assertions of my youth—government is the problem, people who struggle are just lazy, and the successful make it on their own. I now have a deeper respect for the complexities and challenges of modern life. I did not grow up in material prosperity, nor receive an economic head start when my father died as I entered the twenty-first year of life. But I did receive something far more valuable than money—an upbringing rooted in character formation, personal responsibility, and the value of thinking and living well. No price could be placed on such an inheritance.

As I think about the challenges of the twenty-first century in a macro sense, juxtaposed to my own life journey in a micro sense, I am overwhelmed by the burden to focus on this vision of a free and virtuous society. The crass and selfish materialism of our age has failed to meet the material needs of many. It has ignored the deeper pursuit of joy that comes only as the consequence of dignity and meaning. My prayer for all people is that they flourish as they find joy, which is, as C. S. Lewis wrote, "the serious business of heaven."

My friends, this human flourishing is the need of this and every age. Human flourishing is the reward we will enjoy for curing our cultural addiction to blame and overcoming our crisis of responsibility. Our aim and hope is flourishing that leads to joy—and truly takes us home.

ENDNOTES

Chapter 1

1 Strategas Research, "Real US GDP Growth Has Broken From Its Trend Since 2008" (chart).
2 Sean Trende, "Why Trump? Why Now?" *Real Clear Politics*, January 29, 2016, www.realclearpolitics.com/articles/2016/01/29/why_trump _why_now_129486.html.
3 Ibid.
4 Jonah Goldberg, "The Mooch: White House Communications Mis-director," *National Review*, July 28, 2017, www.nationalreview.com /g-file/445477/jeff-sessions-media-bias-donald-trump-age.

Chapter 2

5 President Donald Trump's affection for economic nationalism, and disdain for the impact of freer and more open trade, were by no means unique to the 2015–2016 presidential campaign. The now president was an outspoken critic of free trade and global business evolutions dating as far back as the mid-1980s. The difference: his views were not shared then by either the conservative Right or the liberal Left. Reagan Republicans and Clinton Democrats were both advocates of free trade and the growth benefits of global commerce.

Chapter 3

6 Dennis Prager, "America's Second Civil War," *Townhall*, January 24, 2017, townhall.com/columnists/dennisprager/2017/01/24/americas -second-civil-war-n2275896.
7 Dr. Charles Murray, *Coming Apart: The State of White America, 1960–2010* (New York: Crown Forum, 2012), 154.

8 Pew Research Center, *Analysis of US Decennial Census (1960–2000)*, 2017.

9 United States Census Bureau, *Historical Living Arrangements of Children*, 2014.

10 Robert Lerman, *Marriage and the Economic Well-Being of Families with Children: A Review of the Literature*, Urban Institute and American University, 2002.

11 J. D. Vance, *Hillbilly Elegy: A Memoir and Culture in Crisis* (New York: HarperCollins, 2016), 193.

Chapter 4

12 This hypothetical conversation aligns with multiple accounts of sentiment Fuld expressed in this period, including what has been documented in *A Colossal Failure of Common Sense: The Collapse of Lehman Brothers* by Larry McDonald, pp. 229–231.

13 CoreLogic (previously Baseline Analytics), annual *Mortgage Fraud Report*, 2010.

14 Sumit Agarwal et al., "Predatory Lending and the Subprime Crisis," *Journal of Financial Economics* 113, no. 1 (2014): 29–52.

15 Oliver Wyman, Experian, *Market Intelligence Report*, June 28, 2009.

16 Luigi Guiso, Paola Sapienza, and Luigi Zingales, "Moral and Social Constraints to Strategic Default on Mortgages" (working paper no. 15145, National Bureau of Economic Research, July 2009).

17 Data compiled from www.realtytrac.com, accessed July, 2017.

18 Office of the Comptroller of the Currency and Office of Thrift Supervision, *OCC and OTS Mortgage Metrics Report*, 2009.

19 Ibid.

20 Ben Bernanke, *The Courage to Act: A Memoir of a Crisis and Its Aftermath* (New York: W.W. Norton & Company: 2015), 361.

21 Alt-A lending may be an obnoxious term, but it can best be understood as the sort of middle-ground category of mortgage borrower, with "subprime" primarily referring to those of severalty impaired credit, "prime" referring to those of high credit and financial capability, and "Alt-A" representing the middle ground where the loans would not be conforming to the standards of the government agencies (Fannie and Freddie), hence the term "Alt-A" (i.e., "alternative to the agencies"). These loans often possessed either high debt-to-income ratios or high loan-to-value ratios, but not with the accompanying low FICO score of the subprime category.

22 Darryl E. Getter et al., "Financial Crisis? The Liquidity Crunch of
    August 2007," *Congressional Research Service Report for Congress*,
    September 21, 2007, assets.opencrs.com/rpts/RL34182_20070921.pdf.

23 Alan Greenspan and James Kennedy, "Sources and Uses of Equity
    Extracted from Homes," *Oxford Review of Economic Policy* 24, no. 1
    (2008): 120–144.

Chapter 5

24 Scott Lincicome, "The Truth about Trade," *National Review*, April 4,
    2016.

25 Srikant Devaraj and Dr. Michael Hicks, *The Myth and the Reality
    of Manufacturing in America*, Center for Business and Economic
    Research, Ball State University, 2015.

26 Pablo D. Fajgelbaum and Amit K. Khandelwal, "Measuring the
    Unequal Gains from Trade," *Quarterly Journal of Economics* 131, no. 3
    (August 2016): 1113–1180.

27 Matthew J. Slaughter, "The 'Exporting Jobs' Canard," *Wall Street
    Journal*, June 14, 2017.

28 I might add that within the conservative Right, those apologetics
    have hardly been necessary for most of the last one hundred years.
    Economic nationalism is not only a new phenomenon on the Right,
    but it is essentially a *brand new* phenomenon. The anti-trade wing
    of Republicanism and conservatism has been mostly limited to
    the ilk of Pat Buchannan in recent decades past, whereas 2016
    brought an avalanche of conservatives who suddenly embraced
    a more nationalistic view of trade, either in mere rhetoric or in
    actual policy prescription. Surely the popularity and nomination of
    Donald Trump had a lot to do with this perspective change in many.

29 U.S. Bureau of Labor Statistics, "Job Openings: Total Nonfarm
    (JTSJOL)" (chart), June 2017, fred.stlouisfed.org/series/JTSJOL.

30 Lincicome, "Truth."

Chapter 7

31 Morgan Walsh, "In Defense of School Choice," *Enquiry* IV, no. 17
    (2017).

32 National Education Association, *Rankings & Estimates*, May 2016.

33 "2016 Best and Worst School Systems," WalletHub, August 2016.

34 California Department of Education, *CalEd Facts*, www.cde.ca.gov
    /re/pn/fb/.

35 Troy Senik, "The Worst Union in America," *City Journal*, Spring 2012, www.city-journal.org/html/worst-union-america-13470.html.
36 Ibid.
37 Andrew J. Coulson, "Do Vouchers and Tax Credits Increase Private School Regulation?" (working paper no. 1, Cato Institute, October 4, 2010), object.cato.org/sites/cato.org/files/pubs/pdf/WorkingPaper-1-Coulson.pdf.

Chapter 8

38 Gianmarco Ottaviano and Giovanni Peri, "Re-thinking the Effect of Immigration on Wages," *Journal of the European Economic Association* 10, no. 1 (2011): 152–197.
39 Alex Nowrasteh, "Immigration's Real Impact on Wages and Employment," *At Liberty* (blog), September 15, 2014, www.cato.org/blog/immigrations-real-impact-wages-employment.

Chapter 9

40 "Average Student Loan Debt in America: 2017 Facts & Figures," ValuePenguin, 2017, www.valuepenguin.com/average-student-loan-debt.
41 Emmie Martin, "Student Loan Debt Has Grown 250% in the Last 10 Years—Here's Where Grads Owe the Most," Yahoo Finance, July 19, 2017, finance.yahoo.com/news/student-loan-debt-grown-250-000000611.html.
42 United States Census Bureau, "Current Population Survey," *Annual Social and Economic Supplement*, 2017.
43 Bureau of Labor Statistics, 2010–2016.
44 Charlie Sykes, *Fail U: The False Promise of Higher Education* (New York: St. Martin's Press, 2016).
45 Ibid.

Chapter 10

46 Yuval Levin, *The Fractured Republic: Renewing America's Social Contract in the Age of Individualism*, (New York: Basic Books, 2016), 205.

Chapter 11

47 David Brooks, "The Odyssey Years," *New York Times*, October 9, 2007.

48 Sen. Ben Sasse, *The Vanishing American Adult: Our Coming of Age Crisis and How to Rebuild a Culture of Self-Reliance* (New York: St. Martin's Press, 2017).

49 Jay W. Richards, *Infiltrated: How to Stop the Insiders and Activists Who Are Exploiting the Financial Crisis to Control Our Lives and Our Fortunes* (New York: McGraw Hill, 2013).

Chapter 12

50 Thomas Sowell, *Intellectuals and Society* (New York: Basic Books, 2009), ch. 22.

ACKNOWLEDGMENTS

It really is a justifiable cliché to say that it is impossible to acknowledge all those who deserve acknowledgment for a book.

This book would not have been possible without the love and support of my saintly wife, Joleen, to whom this book is dedicated. And it would not have been possible without a legacy of twenty years (which was about forty years too few) of training, mentoring, parenting, and formation by my late father, Dr. Greg Bahnsen, the greatest intellect I have ever been around. He instilled in me a doctrine of responsibility well before I was ready to hear it.

I am extremely indebted to my publisher, Anthony Ziccardi, my agent, D. J. Snell, my editor, Bill Blankschaen, my publicists, Annie Scranton and Meghan Powers, and the extraordinary team from Post Hill Press. The writing of this book started with a group of people who believed in it and were willing to work with me to bring it to fruition.

My life is filled with a plethora of people I call friends who stimulate my intellectual curiosity and moral imagination. P. Andrew Sandlin, Jeffery J. Ventrella, and Brian G. Mattson at the Center for Cultural Leadership are such men. This message itself would never have been developed in my own mind, let alone have a chance of fertilizing into our society's soil, without the work of Father Robert Sirico and the Acton Institute, where the dream of a free and virtuous society finds foundational support.

My long-time "Triple B" book club partners, Eric Balmer and Aaron Bradford, have been friends for twenty-five years and partnered with me on an incredible reading journey for over a dozen years. Paul Murphy and Brian Harrington have been my sounding boards and discussion partners over many a Manhattan meal working through so many topics. All of these men are dear friends and avenues of support.

My brothers and sisters at Pacifica Christian High School are fighting this good fight with me, teaching kids to think and live well: David and Dayna O'Neil, Keith and Amy Carlson, Michael and Angie Hill, Geoff and Lucie Moore, Scott and Wendy Baugh, Luis and Darcy Garcia, Matt and Catherine Anderson, Chris and Sarah Stratton, and Ben and Cassidy Roberson. Operating leverage in society comes from arming men and women with an appreciation for truth, beauty, and goodness.

For over sixty years there has been an organization standing athwart history yelling, "Stop!" The legacy of William F. Buckley and the continued labors of my friends, mentors, heroes, and colleagues at *National Review* and the National Review Institute are the reason I believe our cause will prevail. Jack Fowler has been a friend to me and a servant to the cause in ways that cannot be articulated. I am in debt to Lindsay Craig, David French, Rich Lowry, Jonah Goldberg, Charlie Cooke, and the entire organization.

I am thankful for my friends in the Lincoln Club of Orange County and all of the conversations and controversies we deal with, many of which made their way into this book. Al Frink, Bob Loewen, Mark Bucher, Michael Capaldi, Kerry Reynolds, John Warner, Wayne Lindholm, Michael Reynolds, Walter Myers, Seth Morrison, Cynthia Quimby—too many more to list. The crisis of responsibility sees its ground zero in our state.

My partners at HighTower Advisors are not only colleagues and friends, but industry visionaries and pioneers committed to a righteous cause. Elliot Weissbluth is a rare breed of leader, a friend, and a disruptor. My life and career have been enhanced by the entire HighTower organization. Thank you to Elliot, Matthias Kuhlmey, Brendan Sullivan, Amit Dogra, Sagar Kurada, Tim Woods, Cheryl Callahan, and all those fighting the fiduciary fight.

Larry Kudlow has impacted me in ways he will never understand, predating the time we even met. I thank Tom Bonds, Brian and Judy Tong, Bob Anderson, John and Michelle Somers, Jim Birchfield, and all who have invested time and love into my well-being.

I can't acknowledge all my Viva boys here because a routine Google search might undermine the whole thesis of the book (kidding, mostly). You are my friends for life.

Thank you to the clients of the Bahnsen Group for giving me the privilege of doing what I love on their behalf. Their faith in our work and intentions comes from trust; and that trust is reciprocated by our undying trustworthiness. I wish I could name every client in this section, not just for their partnership with us, but particularly all those I feel particularly indebted to as friends. Space limitations do not allow. I do thank Mark Corigliano, Tracy Price, Merv Simchowitz, Andrea Shelly, and Stuart Nagasawa for particular levels of support, friendship, and belief.

And I thank my team at the Bahnsen Group—Brian Szytel, Kimberlee Davis, Don Saulic, Brian Tong, Deiya Pernas, Robert Graham, Trevor Cummings, Michelle Leivas, Jacqueline O'Hare, and Peter Van Voorhis—who not only represent the greatest body of client-centric fiduciary advisors I have ever been around, but who are also my partners, friends, and daily allies in the cause of becoming extraordinary.

My family: Kiddos—Mitchell, Sadie, and Graham. Brothers—Jonathan and Mike-Dogg. Extended: Brad, Vicki, Colin, and Monica.

Todd, Joco, and kids. All my in-laws. Quality over Quantity. I love you all.

Finally, I thank the God who loves me, takes care of me, and did for me what I could not do for myself. It is the truth, beauty, and goodness of the creation God made that provokes me to care that a culture rooted in the same be presented to Him.

ABOUT THE AUTHOR

David L. Bahnsen is the Managing Partner of The Bahnsen Group of HighTower Advisors, managing over $1 billion of capital. He is a frequent guest on Fox Business and CNBC, and is annually recognized as one of the top advisors in the country by *Barron's*, *Financial Times*, and others.

For weekly investment commentary and market analysis from David L. Bahnsen:

www.dividendcafe.com